HALF
A MAN

With an Introduction
by Charles Flint Kellogg

American Century Series
HILL AND WANG • NEW YORK

HALF A MAN

The Status

of the Negro

in New York

BY MARY WHITE OVINGTON

TO THE MEMORY OF MY FATHER
THEODORE TWEEDY OVINGTON

Foreword

M ISS OVINGTON'S DESCRIPTION of the status of the Negro in
New York City is based on a most painstaking inquiry into
his social and economic conditions, and brings out in the most
forceful way the difficulties under which the race is laboring, even
in the large cosmopolitan population of New York. It is a refuta-
tion of the claims that the Negro has equal opportunity with the
whites, and that his failure to advance more rapidly than he has
is due to innate inability.

Many students of anthropology recognize that no proof can
be given of any material inferiority of the Negro race; that without doubt the bulk of the individuals composing the race are
equal in mental aptitude to the bulk of our own people; that,
although their hereditary aptitudes may lie in slightly different
directions, it is very improbable that the majority of individuals
composing the white race should possess greater ability than the
Negro race.

The anthropological argument is invariably met by the ob-
jection that the achievements of the two races are unequal, while
their opportunities are the same. Every demonstration of the in-
equality of opportunity will therefore help to dissipate prejudices

that prevent the best possible development of a large number of our citizens.

The Negro of our times carries even more heavily the burden of his racial descent than did the Jew of an earlier period; and the intellectual and moral qualities required to insure success to the Negro are infinitely greater than those demanded from the white, and will be the greater, the stricter the segregation of the Negro community.

The strong development of racial consciousness, which has been increasing during the last century and is just beginning to show the first signs of waning, is the gravest obstacle to the progress of the Negro race, as it is an obstacle to the progress of all strongly individualized social groups. The simple presentation of observations, like those given by Miss Ovington, may help us to overcome more quickly that self-centered attitude which can see progress only in the domination of a single type.

This investigation was carried on by Miss Ovington under the auspices of the Greenwich House Committee on Social Investigations, of which she was a Fellow.

FRANZ BOAS

1911

Contents

Foreword   vii
Introduction by Charles Flint Kellogg   xi

	Introduction 1
CHAPTER ONE	"Up from Slavery" 3
CHAPTER TWO	Where the Negro Lives 17
CHAPTER THREE	The Child of the Tenement 29
CHAPTER FOUR	Earning a Living—Manual Labor and the Trades 41
CHAPTER FIVE	Earning a Living—Business and the Professions 59
CHAPTER SIX	The Colored Woman as a Breadwinner 76
CHAPTER SEVEN	Rich and Poor 93
CHAPTER EIGHT	The Negro and the Municipality 107
CHAPTER NINE	Conclusion 120

Appendix   126

Introduction

No WHITE WOMAN in America has done more in behalf of full
equality for the Negro American than has Mary White
Ovington. Her life exemplifies the greater participation of women
of the progressive era in public affairs and social problems. Like
many of the progressives, she came from the upper middle class—
professional people and intellectuals. Like them she emphasized
change, not through force and violence but through disclosure
of social wrongs, alteration of popular attitudes through education, and redress by orderly legal and democratic processes. The
publication in 1911 of *Half a Man* was the fruition of her ma-
ture experience, study, and thinking on the Negro problem in
New York.

Miss Ovington was unique among women in the progressive
movement in her wholehearted espousal of the cause of the Negro,
which during the age of reform was divorced from other humani-
tarian movements. Jane Addams, Lillian Wald, Florence Kelley,
and Inez Milholland also supported emancipation of the Negro,
but their chief interests lay in other reforms of the day—settlement house work, maternal health, child care, consumers' leagues,
and women's suffrage.

Mary White Ovington was born on April 11, 1865, of a well-to-do family in Brooklyn Heights, New York. The family income was derived from Ovington's, Inc., a Fifth Avenue china and glassware shop founded by her father in 1846. In spite of their wealth and comfortable circumstances, her parents were staunch abolitionists and radicals. Her father had left Plymouth Church in Brooklyn because he felt the pastor, Henry Ward Beecher, was not radical enough on the slavery question, and he joined the small Unitarian church of which his wife was a member.

The maternal grandmother, who lived with the family, was also an ardent abolitionist and a friend of William Lloyd Garrison. She and Garrison's wife had grown up together in Connecticut. She often told the Ovington children tales of abolitionist meetings and of mobs she had encountered. They heard, too, the story of Prudence Crandall, who had lived in a neighboring town and was imprisoned for admitting Negro girls to her school for young ladies. They were taught "to despise Daniel Webster for his Fourth of March speech and Henry Clay for his continual compromising." No wonder that in childhood Mary White Ovington's imagination was stirred by tales of the underground railway and her heroes were the fugitive slaves making their dangerous way to the safety of far-off Canada.

As a young girl, Mary White Ovington devoured the stories of Joel Chandler Harris, Harry Stillwell Edwards, and Thomas Nelson Page which were then appearing in *Century Magazine*. She heard Frederick Douglass speak at Plymouth Church, and came away impressed with the power of his personality. She longed to meet "upper-class Negroes, the descendants, spiritually at least, of the fugitive slaves."

After a "leisurely private school education" at the Brackett School and Packer Collegiate Institute, from which she was graduated in 1890, she spent two years at Radcliffe College, followed by three years of what was then called "going into society" before she turned to a career.

The Radcliffe years (1891–1893) were important ones because it was then that her attitudes toward herself and society matured. Her interest in socialism and labor problems stems from this period. Although she mentions Albert Bushnell Hart and his lecture on slavery and miscegenation in the Old South, it was William J. Ashley, Professor of English Economic History, and Silas MacVane, Professor of Modern European History, who had the greatest influence on her thinking. Her readings on the Peasants' Revolt in England and the French Revolution led her to conclude that history was written from the point of view of the propertied classes, and she determined "to see for [herself] in [her] own city, the life of the working class."

There were no Negro women at Radcliffe during her time, but the following year a Negro girl from Cambridge entered the college, and though Miss Ovington did not know it at the time, W. E. B. Du Bois was at Harvard while she was at Radcliffe. They were not destined to meet for another decade. She later regretted that she had not been privileged to know these students during her college days.

After Radcliffe she worked for a year as registrar at the Pratt Institute, and was then asked by the son of the founder to open the Greenpoint Settlement of the Pratt Institute Neighborhood Association. The Settlement was staffed by students from Pratt Institute's classes in domestic art and science. It was housed in a model brick tenement, "The Astral," named for Charles Pratt's Astral oil refinery, located in the Greenpoint area of Brooklyn. Here Miss Ovington served as headworker from 1895 to 1903. She later spoke of this experience as the best possible preparation for her work with the Negro, for here she learned "that many problems attributed to race are really labor problems."

Miss Ovington left Greenpoint much more of a radical than when she entered upon the work. While at Greenpoint she was elected to the Board of the Social Reform Club on Bond Street, a discussion group predating the popular forum movement in New York. Among the membership of working people and intellectuals were Leonore O'Reilly of the Manhattan Trade School for Girls, Henry Rogers Seager, Professor of Political Economy at Columbia University, and Ernest Crosby, a disciple of Tolstoy.

The Club sponsored reforms for the city, such as the Tenement House Law of 1901, and championed the election of reform mayor Seth Low.

It was not until 1903, her last year at the Greenpoint Settlement, that she became seriously involved in problems of the Negro and race relations. Charles B. Spahr, associate editor of *Outlook* and chairman of the Reform Clubs' program committee, suggested a dinner in honor of Booker T. Washington, whose *Up From Slavery* had appeared in *Outlook*. Miss Ovington took charge of arrangements and, at Spahr's suggestion, provided that a portion of the program deal with the condition of the Negro in New York City. Although she was not impressed with Washington's talk, she was amazed and horrified by a Negro physician's description of discrimination against Negroes and of the worsening conditions in the slums of her own city.

Her college experience, contact with workers in Greenpoint, and discussions at the Social Reform Club had led Miss Ovington to socialism, though several years passed before she joined the party. But it was another dinner meeting of another radical organization to which she belonged that led to her determination to leave Greenpoint to work on problems of the Negro. The organization was the Intercollegiate Socialist Society (later known as the League for Industrial Democracy). The speaker was Lucien Sanial, who had fought with the workers on the barricades of the Paris Commune. In the midst of his address to the group of upper-middle-class, middle-aged people, he warned that unless they repudiated their class they could be of no use to the proletariat. "Even then," he said, "most of you would be useless."

Miss Ovington went home "profoundly disturbed," for she believed that the economic problem of society was of primary importance, but she realized that she was "not of the workers" and was "only cheering and throwing a few pennies." Thus she determined to stop working for socialism and to give her time and energy to securing equality for the Negro, "so that if he chose, he would be able to march with the working class."

By the autumn of 1904, after an attack of typhoid fever and a convalescence in Italy, she was ready for work again. During her illness she had concluded that her best approach to improving race relations was the establishment of a settlement for Negroes. She had read Charles B. Spahr's *The Present Distribution of Wealth in the United States* (1896) and was shocked at the great disparity between the resources of the rich and the poor. She decided that a study of not only the Negro poor of New York, but of all strata of Negro life, was basic to the establishment of such a settlement. As she conceived it, the settlement should not be exclusively for the poor, but should also be a place where middle-class Negroes and whites could meet as equals and discuss topics other than race.

She found an enthusiastic response to her plan in Mrs. Mary Kingsbury Simkhovitch, a fellow student at Radcliffe, who in 1902 with her husband and a group of associates had founded Greenwich House, the first Neighborhood Association in New York City. Miss Ovington knew little about the people with whom she had chosen to work: a Negro population of about 60,000, the most neglected element in the city. Through Professor Simkhovitch, secretary of the Greenwich House committee on social investigations, she was appointed a Greenwich House Fellow for 1904–1905, and was placed under the direction of Professor Seager. At the age of thirty-nine, she was about to begin her lifework.

While resident at Greenwich House she read widely on the Negro problem. She was shocked to discover that most of what was being published about the Negro was rabidly racist and revealed white fear of Negro domination. Many of the old pro-slavery arguments appeared, now stressing biological inferiority, lower brain capacity, and the dangers of race mixture. She felt impelled to refute these writings, but most of the popular magazines, including the muckraking *McClure's,* rejected her material. She did, however, find an outlet in *The Survey* (then known as *Charities and the Commons*), *The Independent,* the *Century,* and the *New York Evening Post,* which under Oswald Garrison Villard's direction was one of the few newspapers sympathetic to the Negro's cause.

Soon after receiving her fellowship, Miss Ovington read an essay from Du Bois' *The Souls of Black Folk* in *Atlantic Monthly.* She at once wrote to him for counsel and advice. Du Bois, who had already published his study on the Negro in Philadelphia, sent helpful suggestions and supplied her with introductions to men and women prominent in the Negro world.

Miss Ovington's awareness of the problems of race in the South began the same year when she visited Hampton Institute, where she met Robert R. Moton and Sarah Forton Grimké. In the spring before the Atlanta riots of 1906, she accepted Du Bois' invitation to attend a sociological conference at Atlanta University. An ugly atmosphere pervaded the city. She met the Negro intelligentsia of Atlanta, and at the same time became familiar with the problems and tensions common to all classes of Negroes in a Southern city.

This was the beginning of a close relationship between Du Bois and Miss Ovington that was to last for thirty years. It seems likely that their friendship was responsible for Du Bois' conversion to socialism. In 1906, representing the *New York Evening Post,* she reported on the second convention of Du Bois' Niagara Movement at Harper's Ferry. Afterward Du Bois asked her to join the Movement, which he had founded in 1905 to arouse the Negro elite to lead agitation for full political and civil rights. She immediately accepted and tried to persuade him to permit her to address the 1908 meeting on the relationship of the Negro to the labor question.

Both Miss Ovington and Du Bois served on the Board of Directors of the biracial Constitutional League of the United States, founded in 1903 by reformer-philanthropist John E. Milholland. When the NAACP was organized, it was natural that Miss Ovington and the other radicals should propose Du Bois as chief executive of the organization. Villard and the conservatives objected, and a compromise was reached by which Du Bois was brought in as Director of Publicity and Research. Until Du Bois' withdrawal from the NAACP in 1934, Miss Ovington on most occasions loyally supported him in his many clashes with his colleagues and fellow Board members.

During the winter of 1906–1907, Miss Ovington again went South to expand her knowledge of the Negro world. Because Negroes were migrating to New York and other Northern urban centers, she felt it was essential to her survey for *Half a Man* to familiarize herself with the Southern environment from which they came. In Atlanta she saw the devastation caused by the race riots and felt the bitterness of the Negro community. She visited Tuskegee Institute and other rural industrial schools in the Deep South, or "darkest America," where wrongs against the people of color were so depressing.

An introduction from Milholland led her to visit with the Joseph C. Mannings, a white family living in a small town in Alabama. Manning was a former member of the Alabama legislature who edited a country newspaper, the *Southern American.* He held the postmastership of Alexander City by virtue of membership in the Republican party. He and his family were ostracized by the white community and were eventually forced to leave the South because he dared to publish material favorable to the Negro. Manning revealed many of the indignities heaped upon Negroes in the rural South and one of these episodes formed the basis of Miss Ovington's short story "The White Brute."

En route to Birmingham she visited a typical Piedmont upland county, where there were few Negroes, and found stark poverty and rampant Negrophobia. In Birmingham she conferred with the Alabama state secretary of the Socialist party as a semiofficial representative of the New York State Central Committee. This conference gave her an insight into the difficulty of organizing Negro and white workers because of racial antagonisms.

Having visited the Black Belt, the Piedmont, and the urban South, she returned to New York filled with despair. Her family persuaded her to travel abroad, but even there she concentrated on observing the condition of the working class in Europe.

Back in New York she spent the winter of 1907–1908 living in a Negro tenement, "The Tuskegee," hard at work on her survey. The Tuskegee, located on West Sixty-third Street near Eleventh Avenue, was at the northern edge of a Negro district known as San Juan Hill. This model tenement had been built by Henry Phipps as a result of the combined efforts of Miss Ovington and John E. Milholland to interest him in an experiment in model housing for Negroes. Up to this time Phipps's attention had been concentrated on alleviating housing conditions among white slum dwellers.

Since the settlement in Greenpoint had been housed in The Astral, also a model tenement, Miss Ovington hoped to start her settlement work for Negroes in The Tuskegee. She was unable, however, to obtain Phipps's permission to carry on social work in his tenement and so had to give up the idea of a settlement for Negroes in Manhattan. Three years had now been spent in gathering material for *Half a Man*. The fellowship had run out and still the book was not finished.

She returned to Brooklyn and joined with Verina Morton-Jones, one of the first Negro women physicians in the United States, in founding the Lincoln Settlement for Negroes. Miss Ovington recruited its Board of Directors, became its chairman, and raised the money for its support. Dr. Morton-Jones served as headworker. Then came the Cosmopolitan Club dinner, the aftermath of which nearly wrecked the settlement.

The Cosmopolitan Club had been founded in 1906 as an interracial organization concerned with correcting misinformation about the Negro and bridging the gulf between Negroes and whites. It met from time to time in the homes of Brooklyn's well-to-do Negro families such as the George Wibecans and the Owen M. Wallers. Wibecan was a newspaperman and Waller a physician and member of the Niagara Movement.

In the spring of 1908, at Miss Ovington's suggestion, the Cosmopolitan Club held an interracial dinner at Peck's Restaurant on lower Fulton Street. Dr. Waller presided. Nearly one hundred clergy, social workers, and professional persons attended, including such distinguished white persons as Hamilton Holt, editor of *The Independent,* John Spargo, the socialist writer and lecturer, and Oswald Garrison Villard. Among those prominent in the Negro world were the Reverend Fraser Miller, Rector of St. Augustine's Church in Brooklyn, and the Reverend William H. Ferris, teacher and lecturer.

News of New York's first interracial dinner was leaked in advance to the press, whose representatives appeared at the dinner, took photographs, and the following day poured forth a torrent of abuse concerning the "orgy." According to the papers, "socialist propaganda" was the force of evil behind this "sordid event." Their principal target was Miss Ovington. When the Brooklyn papers took up the matter, the outcry against her was so great, and the threats of withdrawal of support from the Lincoln Settlement were so many, that she and the Board had to give assurances against any repetition in order to insure the continuance of the Settlement.

Eventually support of the Lincoln Settlement was taken over by the Urban League (The National League on Urban Conditions Among Negroes). Miss Ovington was a founder and sponsor of two of the three original groups which merged in 1911 to form the League. At meetings of these organizations, which concerned themselves with work opportunities and social problems facing Negroes in New York City, she "met new people both white and colored" and obtained valuable information for her project.

Meantime, while still living at The Tuskegee, she took the leadership in the founding of the NAACP. From its very beginning in 1909, until her retirement in 1947 at the age of eighty-two, Miss Ovington was a moving spirit within the NAACP. She was a formulator and signer of the "Call" for a national organization, a member of the National Committee of Forty, a member of the Program Committee, the Executive Committee, an incorporator, and a member of the New York Vigilance Committee of the Association. Twice she was its secretary, twice the chairman of its Board of Directors. She at one period held the position of Director of Branches and at the time of her retirement was treasurer of the National Association.

At about the time of the incorporation of the NAACP in 1911, *Half a Man: The Status of the Negro in New York* was published. The study was the culmination of seven years of intelligent, sympathetic, and keen observation of the Negro not only in New York, but in the urban and rural South as well. During the time that Miss Ovington had lived in the Negro tenement, working with women and children, she had accompanied tenement house inspectors through many of the old-law buildings of the district. She supplemented this direct knowledge and experience with data secured from the files of the Department of Health, from the Juvenile Court Records, the United States Census, and other official sources.

Out of her unique experiences during these years she developed an empathy for the Negro and an unusual understanding of the disabilities he suffered because of color. Du Bois maintained that all relationships between black and white broke along the "color line," and that color was the basis of friction and trouble between the races. Even people who thought of themselves as liberal and unprejudiced were often subconsciously biased. Their words and actions revealed a hidden hostility or an insulting paternalism. This is what black militants today mean when they accuse a person or an institution of racism. Du Bois found Miss Ovington free of any shadow of the "color line." This was high praise from one who was sensitive to the slightest shade of racism.

It might seem that the founder of a radical organization dedicated to the achievement of full-citizenship status for a despised minority could not treat her subject in a scholarly and objective manner, but such is not the case. Much of the impact of *Half a Man* lies in the combination of sound scholarship, discriminating use of material, and a delightful style enlivened by wit and humor. Miss Ovington was not a fanatic or bitter partisan. In *Half a Man* she condemns no one and offers no solutions. She gently and quietly sets down all the injustice, all the cruelty and hatred, all the stupidity and hypocrisy inherent in racism.

The book is significant in that the problems it enumerates concerning the plight of the Negro are still to be found in cities across the nation. Then, as now, the Negro was confronted with segregated and deteriorated housing, high rent, overcrowding, poverty, inferior educational facilities, malnutrition, unstable home life, working mothers, crime, juvenile delinquency, and limited opportunities for work and recreation. These conditions were common to American cities North as well as South, and bear witness to the fact that the Negro has been cut off from participation in many of the benefits of American civilization. The revolution of the nineteen-sixties underscores the impatience of Negroes with the slow pace of change. Though the "Black Bourgeoisie" has grown in numbers and influence, the masses of the Negro population in the urban ghettos still live in conditions scarcely, if at all, better than those of 1911.

All of Miss Ovington's published works reflect her interest in Negroes. Her experiences with the children of the Negro tenement districts of Manhattan and Brooklyn made her realize the paucity of literature suitable for Negro children, and she wrote three books which were pioneer works in meeting the longing of Negro children for stories of their own people and instilling a sense of worth and pride in their race.

In 1920 she wrote *The Shadow,* a novel of the race problem and the labor movement, which was serialized in England and Ireland as well as in the Negro press in America. In *Portraits in Color* (1927) she sketched the life and work of twenty distinguished Negroes, men and women, presenting them as human beings of value and dignity.

Her autobiographical work, *The Walls Came Tumbling Down* (1947), is the story of the NAACP and a courageous woman of culture and refinement, "a fighting saint," who gave herself to the desperate needs of the Negro American. During her last years with the NAACP, when she was ill and in straitened circumstances, she could no longer donate her services. The NAACP, in gratitude to "the Mother of the New Emancipation," gave her a small salary. She died in 1951, at the age of eighty-six, forty years after *Half a Man* was published.

In 1911, Miss Ovington had been optimistic concerning future progress in race relations. The restraints preventing the Negro's achievement of full manhood were not due to his incapacity, but to the artificial barriers imposed upon him by white society. The stereotypes resulting from the classification of Negroes in terms of the group rather than as individuals and the psychological devastation caused by their treatment as inferiors contributed to the turmoil, confusion, and loss of identity within the Negro world. Although she offered no concrete solutions, Miss Ovington saw, as one sharing the vision of the progressive era, that an enlarged social consciousness on the part of the white community, together with the provision of greater opportunities for education and participation as citizens, would be essential for the removal of artificial barriers to the Negro's emancipation.

She anticipated that much of New York's "provincialism," with its attendant prejudice, would be diluted by immigration from non-Anglo-Saxon countries—but even as her book came off the press, in Coatesville, Pennsylvania, a town inhabited by large numbers of recent immigrants, a Negro was burned alive. The history of the immigrant has been that he has conformed to the racial mores of America instead of transforming them. It was psychologically elevating for immigrants entering the United States during this period to find the Negro beneath them.

Although the barriers erected by labor unions are falling, "last hired and first fired" is still a reality for the Negro labor force. Police brutality is still a source of friction. Although Negroes are being hired as policemen, the Negro ghetto dweller today considers this as mere tokenism; he looks upon officers of the law as members of an invading army and on the courts as instruments of white exploitation and oppression. It has taken rioting and burning in the cities to bring about a consideration of the concept of "black capitalism" as a possible solution to the lack of opportunities for Negroes in the business world. Advertising and television are now helping to overcome the stereotypes fostered for many years in the entertainment world.

The barriers to the attainment of full-manhood status are crumbling but the walls still have not "tumbled down." It is significant that sixty years after the appearance of the title *Half a Man,* the American Negro still feels impelled to use the term "MAN," to reinforce in himself and upon white consciousness the concept of his manhood, and to replace other infuriating, degrading, and insulting appellations. The tardy awakening of the white community is in itself an advance making possible the replacement of race repression with changed attitudes of the majority group, intelligent social planning, and full extension of political and economic democracy.

CHARLES FLINT KELLOGG

May, 1969

The research for this introduction was done under grants from the Penrose Fund of the American Philosophical Society and the Division of Research and Publication of the National Endowment for the Humanities.

C.F.K.

HALF
A MAN

HALF
A MAN

Introduction

SIX YEARS AGO I met a young colored man, a college student recently returned from Germany where he had been engaged in graduate work. He was born, he told me, in one of the Gulf States, and I questioned him as to whether he intended going back to the South to teach. His answer was in the negative. "My father has attained success in his native state," he said, "but when I ceased to be a boy, he advised me to live in the North where my manhood would be respected. He himself cannot continually endure the position in which he is placed, and in the summer he comes North to be a man. No," correcting himself, "to be half a man. A Negro is wholly a man only in Europe."

Half a man! During the six years that I have been in touch with the problem of the Negro in New York this characterization has grown in significance to me. I have endeavored to know the life of the Negro as I know the life of the white American, and I have learned that while New York at times gives full recognition to his manhood, again, its race prejudice arrests his development as certainly as severe poverty arrests the development of the tenement child. Perhaps a study of this shifting attitude on the part of the dominant race, and of the Negro's reaction under it, may not be unimportant; for the color question cannot be ignored in America, nor should the position taken by her largest city be overlooked. And those who love their fellows may be glad, among New York's four millions—its Slavs and Italians, its Russians and Asiatics—to meet these dark people who speak our language and who for many generations have made this country their home.

CHAPTER ONE

"Up from Slavery"

THE STATUS of the Negro in New Amsterdam, a slave in a pioneer community, differed fundamentally from his position today in New York. His history from the seventeenth to the twentieth century contains many exciting incidents, but those only need be considered here that show a progress or a retardation in his attainment to manhood. What were his struggles in the past to secure his rights as a man?

Slavery in the early days of the colonies was more brutal than at the time of final emancipation. Savages recently arrived from Africa lacked the docility of blacks reared in bondage, and burning and torturing, as well as whipping, were recognized modes of punishment. Masters looked upon their Negroes, bought at the Wall Street market from among the cargo of a recently arrived slaver, with some suspicion and fear. Nor were their apprehensions entirely without reason. In 1712 some of the discontented among the New York slaves met in an orchard in Maiden Lane and set fire to an outhouse. Defending themselves against the citizens who ran to put out the flames, they fired, killing nine men and wounding six. Retribution soon followed. They were pursued when they attempted flight, captured and

3

executed—some hanged, some burned at the stake, some left suspended in chains to starve to death.

Perhaps it was the memory of this small revolt that caused the people of New York in 1741 to lay the blame for a series of conflagrations upon their slaves. Nine fires that seemed to be incendiary came one upon another, and a robbery was committed. To escape death herself, a worthless white servant girl gave testimony against the Negroes who frequented a tavern where she was employed, declaring that a plot had been conceived whereby the slaves would kill all the white men and take control of the city. New York was aflame with fear, and evidence that at another time would have been rejected, was listened to by the judges with grave attention. The slaves were allowed no defense, and before the city had recovered from its fright, it had burned fourteen Negroes, hanged eighteen, and transported seventy-one.[1]

Historians today think that the slaves were in no way concerned in this so-called "plot." The two thousand blacks in the city might have done such mischief to the ten thousand whites, but their servile condition made an organized movement among them impossible. We may infer, however, from the fear which they provoked, that they were not all docile servants. In a letter written at the port of New York in 1756, an English naval officer says of the city, "The laborious people in general are Guinea Negroes who lie under particular restraints from the attempts they have made to massacre the inhabitants for their liberty." [2] Janvier in his "Old New York" thinks, "that the alarm bred by the so-called Negro plot of 1741 was most effective in checking the growth of slavery in that city." Probably the restlessness of the slaves, their efforts toward manhood, in a community where there was little economic justification for slavery, contributed to the movement for emancipation that began in 1777.

1. Daniel Horsmanden, *New York Conspiracy, or a History of the Negro Plot.*
2. James Grant Wilson, *History of New York,* Vol. II, p. 314.

Emancipation came gradually to the New York Negro. Gouverneur Morris at the state constitutional convention of 1776–1777 recommended that "the future legislature of the state of New York take the most effectual measures consistent with the public safety and the private property of individuals for abolishing domestic slavery within the same, so that in future ages every human being who breathes the air of this state shall enjoy the privileges of a freeman." The postponement of action to a future legislature was keenly regretted by John Jay, who was absent from the convention when the slavery question arose, but who had hoped that New York might be a leader in emancipation. The state's initial measure for abolishing slavery was in 1785, when it prohibited the sale of slaves in New York. This was followed in 1799 by an act giving freedom to the children of slaves, and in 1817 by a further act providing for the abolition of slavery throughout the state in 1827. This law went into effect July 4, 1827, the emancipation day of the Negroes in New York.

With gradual emancipation and the cessation of the sale of slaves, the Negroes numerically became unimportant in the city. In 1800 they constituted 10.5 per cent of the population. Half a century later, while they had doubled their numbers, the immense influx of foreign immigrants brought their proportion down to 2.7 per cent. In 1850 and 1860 their positive as well as their relative number decreased, and it was not until twenty years ago that they began to show some gain. The last census returns of 1900 give Greater New York (including Brooklyn) 60,666 Negroes in a population of 3,437,202, 1.8 per cent. It seems probable that the census of 1910 will show a large positive and a slight relative Negro increase.

The relative decrease in the number of Negroes did not, however, produce a decrease in the agitation upon their presence and position in the city. Their political status was a subject for heated discussion even before their complete emancipation. The first state constitution, drafted in 1777, was without color discrimination, since it based the suffrage upon a property qualification requiring voters for Governor and Senators to be freeholders owning property worth £100. A Negro with such a holding was a phenomenon, a curiosity. But by 1821, when the framing of the second constitution was in progress, Negroes of some education were an appreciable element in the population,

POPULATION OF NEW YORK FROM 1800 TO 1900:
TOTAL AND NEGRO

	BOROUGH OF MANHATTAN		
	Total	Negro	Percentage of Negroes
1800	60,515	6,382	10.5
1810	96,373	9,823	10.2
1820	123,706	10,886	8.8
1830	202,589	13,976	6.9
1840	312,710	16,358	5.2
1850	515,547	13,815	2.7
1860	805,658	12,574	1.6
1870	942,292	13,072	1.5
	BOROUGHS OF MANHATTAN AND BRONX		
1880	1,206,299	19,663	1.6
1890	1,515,301	23,601	1.6
1900	2,050,600	38,616	1.9
	GREATER NEW YORK		
1900	3,437,202	60,666	1.8

and with them ignorant, recently emancipated slaves. Should they be admitted to the full manhood suffrage contemplated for the whites? Those who favored the new democratic movement were doubtful of its applicability to colored people. Livingston, a champion of universal white manhood suffrage, was against giving the black man the vote. On the other hand, the conservative Chancellor Kent, apprehending in the new constitution "a disposition to encroach on private rights,—to disturb chartered privileges and to weaken, degrade, and overawe the administration of justice," would yet have made no color discrimination, and Peter A. Jay, who did not believe in universal white manhood suffrage, urged that colored men, natives of the country, should derive from its institutions the same privileges as white persons. The second constitution when adopted enfranchised practically all white men, but gave the Negroes a property qualification of $250. The issue of the revolution, however, was not far from men's thoughts, and "taxation without representation" was not permitted; for while no colored man might vote without a freehold estate valued at $250, *no person of color was subject to direct taxation unless he should be possessed of such real estate.*

In 1846 a third constitutional convention was held, and the same matter came up for debate. John L. Russell of St. Lawrence declared that "the Almighty had created the black man inferior to the white man," while Daniel S. Waterbury of Delaware County believed that "the argument that because a race of men is marked by a peculiarity of color and crooked hair they are not endowed with a mind equal to another class who have other peculiarities is unworthy of men of sense." John H. Hunt of New York City proclaimed that "We want no masters, least of all no Negro masters. . . . Negroes are aliens." And he predicted that the practical effect of their admission to the suffrage would be their exclusion from Manhattan Island. A delegation of colored men appeared at Albany before the suffrage committee, but their arguments and those of their friends produced no effect. The new constitution contained the same Negro property qualification, and it was not until 1874, after the passage of the fifteenth amendment to the Constitution of the United States, that legislation placed the Negro voter of New York upon the same footing as the white.[3]

Had New York sincerely desired to keep the Negro in an inferior position, it could have accomplished this by refusing him an education. This it never did, though it suffered much tribulation regarding the place and manner of his instruction. Before the establishment of a public school system, the Manumission society, an association composed largely of Friends, though including in its membership John Jay, De Witt Clinton, and Alex-

3. For a full account of the Negro's political status in New York consult Charles Z. Lincoln's *Constitutional History of New York.*

ander Hamilton, undertook the education of the Negro. In 1787 it opened a school for Africans on Cliff Street. One of the early teachers was Charles C. Andrews, whose little book on *The African Free Schools,* published in 1830, shows a kindly tolerance for the black race. "As a result of forty years' experience," he writes, "the idea respecting the capacity of the African race to receive a respectable and even a liberal education has not been visionary." And he recites the names of some of his pupils: "Rev. Theodore S. Wright, graduate of Princeton Theological Seminary; John B. Russworm, graduate of Bowdoin; Edward Jones, graduate of Amherst; William Brown and William G. Smith, students of the medical department, Columbia College: all of them persons of color." Describing an annual exhibition of his school on May 12, 1824, he quotes from the *Commercial Advertiser* of the same date: "We never beheld a white school, of the same age (of and under the age of fifteen), in which, without exception, there was more order and neatness of dress and cleanliness of person. And the exercises were performed with a degree of promptness and accuracy which was surprising."

In 1834 the public-school association took over the schools of the Manumission society, but before this time the Negroes had begun to assert themselves regarding the method and place of instruction for their children. They clamored for colored teachers and succeeded in displacing Charles Andrews himself. In 1838, at their desire, the word African was changed to colored in describing the race; but of chief importance to their educational future, they began a protest, only to end in 1900, against segregation.

Removed from the care of the Manumission society, the colored schools deteriorated. Their grade was reduced,[4] and owing to the growth of the city, their attendance was very irregular, the severe winter weather often keeping children who lived at a distance at home. A Brooklyn man tells me that, when a boy, he used to walk from his home at East New York to Fulton Ferry, passing inferior

4. Thomas Boese, *Public Education in the City of New York,* p. 227.

Brooklyn colored schools, and after crossing the river, on up to Mulberry Street to be instructed by the popular colored teacher, John Peterson. Here he received a good education; but few boys would have endured a daily trip of fourteen miles. Increasingly parents, if the colored school of their neighborhood was not of the best, sent their boys and girls to be instructed with the white boys and girls of their district.

The state law declared that any city or incorporated village might establish separate schools for the instruction of African youths, provided the facilities were equal to those of white schools, and when, in 1862, a colored parent brought a case against the city for forcing her child to go to a colored school, the case was lost.[5] Nevertheless, during the nineteenth century Negroes in some numbers attended white schools in both Brooklyn and New York, and Negro parents continued in their quiet but persistent efforts against segregation. Then again, New York grew too rapidly to segregate any race. The Negro boys and girls were scattered through many districts, and the attendance at colored schools fell off; in 1879 it was less than in 1878, and in 1880 less than in 1879; so that the Board of Education in 1883 decided to disestablish three colored schools.

But this involved another factor. If the colored schools were disestablished, what would become of the colored teachers? The Negroes met this issue by delaying disestablishment for a year, while the teachers went about among the parents of the ward, making friends and urging that children, *white or colored,* be sent to their schools. Numbers of new pupils of both races were brought in within the year, and at the end of the time, after a hearing before the Governor, then Grover Cleveland, a bill was passed prohibiting the abolition of two of the three colored schools, but also making them open to all children regardless of color.[6]

Occasionally a colored girl graduated from the normal college of the city, but if there was no vacancy for her in the four colored

5. King *v.* Gallagher, 1882.
6. A. Emerson Palmer, *The New York Public School.*

schools she received no appointment. In 1896, however, a normal graduate, Miss S. E. Frazier, insisted upon her right to be appointed as teacher in any school in which there was a vacancy. She visited the ward trustees and the members of the Board of Education, and represented to them the injustice done her and her race in refusing her the chance to prove her ability as a teacher in the first school that should need a normal graduate. She was finally appointed to a position in a white school. Her success with her pupils was immediate, and since then the question of race or color has not been considered in the appointment of teachers in New York.

Until 1900, the state law permitted the establishment of separate colored schools. In that year, however, on the initiative of Theodore Roosevelt, then Governor, the legislature passed a bill providing that no person should be refused admission or be excluded from any public school in the state on account of race or color.[7] This closed the question of compulsory segregation in the state, though before this it had ceased in New York. Public education was thus democratized for the New York Negroes, their persistent efforts bringing at the end complete success.

While the colored people in New York started with segregated schools and attained to mixed schools, the movement in the churches was the reverse. At first the Negroes were attendants of white churches, sitting in the gallery or on the rear seats, and waiting until the white people were through before partaking of the communion; but as their number increased they chafed under their position. Why should they be placed apart to hear the doctrine of Christ, and why, too, should they not have full opportunity to preach that doctrine? The desire for self-expression was perhaps the greatest factor in leading them to separate from the white church. In 1796 about thirty Negroes, under the leadership of James Varick,[8] withdrew from the John Street Methodist Episcopal Church, and formed the first colored church of New

7. Laws of New York, Chapter 492.
8. B. F. Wheeler, D.D., *The Varick Family*.

York. Varick had been denied a license to preach, but now as pastor of his own people, he was recognized by the whites and helped by some of them. He was the founder of the African Methodist Episcopal Zion Church.

The Abyssinian Baptist Church was organized in 1800 by a few colored members who withdrew from the First Baptist Church, then in Gold Street, to establish themselves on Worth Street,[9] and in 1818 the colored Episcopalians organized St. Philip's Church. In 1820 one of their race, Peter Williams, for six years deacon, became their preacher.

Another prominent church was the colored Congregational, situated, in 1854, on Sixth Street; and it was the determined effort of its woman organist to reach the church in time to perform her part in the Sunday morning service that led to an important Negro advance in citizenship.

In the middle of the last century the right of the Negro to ride in car or omnibus depended on the sufferance of driver, conductor, and passenger. Sometimes a car stopped at a Negro's signal, again the driver whipped up his horses, while the conductor yelled to the "nigger" to wait for the next car. Entrance might always be effected if in the company of a white person, and the small child of a kindly white household would be delegated to accompany the homeward bound black visitor into her car where, after a few minutes, conductor and passengers having become accustomed to her presence, the young protector might slip away. Such a situation was very galling to the self-respecting Negro.

In July, 1854, Elizabeth Jennings, a colored schoolteacher and organist at the Congregational Church, attempted to board a Third Avenue car at Pearl and Chatham streets. She was hurrying to reach the church to perform her part in the service. The conductor stopped, but as Miss Jennings mounted the platform, he told her that she must wait for the next car, which was reserved for her people. "I have no people," Miss Jennings said.

9. George H. Hansell, *Reminiscences of New York Baptists.*

"I wish to go to church as I have for six months past, and I do not wish to be detained." The altercation continued until the car behind came up, and the driver there declaring that he had less room than the car in front, the woman was grudgingly allowed to enter the car. "Remember," the conductor said, "if any passenger objects, you shall go out, whether or no, or I'll put you out."

"I am a respectable person, born and brought up in New York," said Miss Jennings, "and I was never insulted so before."

This again aroused the conductor. "I was born in Ireland," he said, "and you've got to get out of this car."

He attempted to drag her out. The woman clung to the window, the conductor called in the driver to help him, and together they dragged and pulled and at last threw her into the street. Badly hurt, she nevertheless jumped back into the car. The driver galloped his horses down the street, passing every one until a policeman was found who pushed the woman out, not, however, until she had taken the number of the car. She then made her way home.

Elizabeth Jennings took the case into court, and it came before the Supreme Court of the State in February, 1855, Chester A. Arthur, afterwards President of the United States, being one of the lawyers for the plaintiff. The judge's charge was clear on the point that common carriers were bound to carry all respectable people, white or colored, and the plaintiff was given $225 damages, to which the court added 10 per cent and costs; and to quote the *New York Tribune*'s comment on the case,[10] "Railroads, steamboats, omnibuses, and ferryboats will be admonished from this as to the rights of respectable colored people." [11]

When you talk with the elderly educated colored people of New York today, they tell you that before the war were "dark days." The responsibility felt by the thoughtful Negroes was very

10. *New York Tribune,* February 23, 1855.

11. "The Story of an Old Wrong," in *The American Woman's Journal,* July, 1895.

great. They had not only their own battles to wage, but there were the fugitives who were entering the city by the Underground Railroad, whom they must assist though it cost them their own liberty. In 1835 a Vigilance Committee was formed in New York City to take charge of all escaping slaves, and also to prevent the arrest and return to slavery of free men of color. Colored men served on this committee, and its secretary was the minister of the church to which Elizabeth Jennings was endeavoring to make her way that Sunday morning, the Reverend Charles B. Ray. In 1850 the New York State Vigilance Committee was formed with Gerritt Smith as President and Ray as Secretary. Ray's home was frequently used to shelter fugitives.[12] Once a young man, stepping up to the door and learning that it was Charles Ray's house, whistled to his companions in the darkness, and fourteen black men made their appearance and received shelter. There would also come the task of negotiating for the purchase of a slave, or this proving impossible, for the careful working out of a means for his escape. Dark days, indeed, but made memorable to the Negro by heroic work and the friendship of great men. Perhaps the two races have never worked together in such fine companionship as at the unlawful and thrilling task of protecting and aiding the fugitive.

The hardest year of the century for the Negro was 1863, when the draft riot imperiled every dark face. Many Negroes fled from the city. Colored homes were fired, the Orphan Asylum for colored children on Fifth Avenue was burned, and even the dead might not be buried save at the peril of undertaker and priest. Elizabeth Jennings, now Mrs. Graham, lost a child when the rioting was at its height. An undertaker named Winterbottom, a white man, was brave enough to give his services, winning the lasting gratitude and patronage of the colored people. With the danger of violence about them, the father and mother went to Greenwood Cemetery, where the Reverend Morgan Dix of Trinity Church read the burial service at the grave.

12. Life of the Reverend Charles B. Ray.

With the end of the war and the passage of the fourteenth and fifteenth amendments came a revulsion of feeling for the race. "I remember," an old-time friend of the Negro tells me, "when the fifteenth amendment was passed. The colored people stood in great numbers on the streets, and on their faces was a look of gratitude and thanksgiving that I shall never forget." Following the amendment came the State Civil Rights Bill in 1873, declaring that all persons should be entitled to full and equal accommodations in all public places; and discrimination for a time largely ceased.

While the colored people were winning citizenship, their progress in industry was also considerable. Until 1860 the race was infrequently segregated, and black and white were neighbors, not only in their homes, but in business. Samuel R. Scottron, a careful Negro writer, compiled a long list of the trades in which Negroes engaged before the war. Besides the various lines of domestic service, in which they were more frequently seen than today—coachmen, cooks, waitresses, seamstresses, barbers—there were many craftsmen, ship-builders, trimmers, riggers, coopers, caulkers, printers, tailors, carpenters. "Second-hand clothing shops were everywhere kept by colored men. All the caterers and restaurant keepers of the high order, as well as small places, were kept by colored men. . . . Varick and Peters kept about the most pretentious barber shop in the city. Patrick Reason was one of the most capable engravers. The greatest among the restaurateurs was Thomas Downing, who kept a restaurant under what is now the Drexel Building, corner of Wall and Broad streets. The drug stores of Dr. James McCune Smith on West Broadway, and Dr. Philip A. White on Frankfort Street, were not outclassed by any kept by white men in their day." [13]

And so the list goes on. It is perhaps somewhat exaggerated in the importance in the city's business life which it gives to the colored race. Charles Andrews, in 1837, says of the pupil who graduates from his school, "He leaves with every avenue closed

13. *Colored American Magazine*, October, 1907.

against him—doomed to encounter as much prejudice and contempt as if he were not only destitute of that education which distinguishes the civilized from the savage, but as if he were incapable of receiving it." And he goes on to tell of those few who have been able to learn trades, and their subsequent difficulties in finding employment in good shops. White journeymen object to working in the same shop with them, and many of the best lads go to sea or become waiters, barbers, coachmen, servants, laborers. But he is writing of an early date, and the opinion of the colored people seems to be that, before our large foreign immigration, the Negro was more needed in New York than today and received a large share of satisfactory employment. His chief competitor was the Irish immigrant, like himself an agricultural laborer, without previous training in business, and he was frequently able to hold his own in his shop. His long experience in domestic service, moreover, made him a better caterer than the representatives of any other nationality that had yet entered the city. His churches were flourishing, thus securing a profession for which he had natural ability, and as we have seen, colored men and women taught in the New York schools.

The city grew rapidly after 1875, and the colored society, the little group that had attained to modest means and education, bought homes, chiefly in Brooklyn, where land was easier to secure than in Manhattan, and strove to enlarge the opportunities for those who were to come after them. Color prejudice had waned, and they often met with especial consideration because of their race. Had they been white they would have slipped into the population and been lost, as happened to the Germans and the Irish, who had been their competitors. As it was, they formed a society apart from the rest of the city, meeting it occasionally in work or through the friendship of children, who, left to themselves, know no race. They had battled against prejudice and had won their rights as citizens.

As we look at the life of a segregated people, however, we see that we tend always to regard not the individual but the group. The Negro is a man in Europe, because there he is an individual, standing or falling by his own merits. But in America, even in so cosmopolitan a city as New York, he is judged, not by his own achievements, but by the achievements of every other New York black man. So we will leave these able colored Americans, who won much both for themselves and for their race, and turn to the mass of the Negroes, the toiling poor, who dwell in our tenements today.

CHAPTER TWO

Where the
Negro Lives

I IS THIRTY-FIVE YEARS since, in his "Symphony," Sidney Lanier told of

> The poor
> That stand by the inward opening door
> Trade's hand doth tighten evermore,
> And sigh their monstrous foul air sigh
> For the outside hills of liberty.

Were Lanier writing this today, we should wonder whether New York's crowded tenements had not served as inspiration for his figure. The island of Manhattan, about eight miles long by two miles wide, with an additional slender triangle of five miles at the north end, in 1905, housed two million one hundred and twelve thousand people. These men and women and children were not scattered uniformly throughout the island, but were placed in selected corners, one thousand to the acre, while a mile or so away large comfortable homes held families of two or three. This was Manhattan's condition in 1905, and with each

17

succeeding year more congestion takes place, and more pressure is felt upon the inward opening door.[1]

The Negro with the rest of the poor of New York has his part in this excessive overcrowding. The slaver in which he made his entrance to this land provided in floor space six feet by one-foot-four for a man, five feet by one-foot-four for a woman, and four feet by one-foot-four for a child.[2] This outdoes any overcrowding New York can produce, but an ever increasing cost in food and rent is bringing into her interior bedrooms a mass of humanity approximating that of the slaver's ship. These newcomers, however, are not unwilling occupants, since unlike the slaves they may spend their day and much of their night amid an ocean of changing and exciting incidents. If you are young and strong, you care less where you sleep than where you may spend your waking hours.

From among the millions of New York's poor, can we pick out the Negroes in their tenements? This is not so difficult a task as it would have proved fifty years ago when the colored were scattered throughout the city; today we find them confined to fairly definite quarters. A black face on the lower East Side is viewed with astonishment, while on the middle West Side it is no more noticeable than it would be in Atlanta or New Orleans. Roughly we may count five Negro neighborhoods in Manhattan: Greenwich Village, the middle West Side, San Juan Hill, the upper East Side, and the Upper West Side. Brooklyn has a large Negro population, but it is more widely distributed and less easily located than that of Manhattan.

Of the five Manhattan neighborhoods the oldest is Greenwich Village, according to Janvier once the most attractive part of New York, where the streets "have a tendency to sidle away from each other and to take sudden and unreasonable turns." Here one finds such fascinating names as Minetta Lane and Carmine and Cornelia streets. These and neighboring thoroughfares grow daily more grimy, however, and no longer merit Jan-

---

1. Harold M. Finley in *Federation*, May, 1908.
2. Thomas Clarkson, *History of the Abolition of the Slave Trade*, p. 378.

vier's praise for cleanliness, moral and physical. The picturesque, friendly old houses are giving way to factories with high, monotonous fronts, where foreigners work who crowd the ward and destroy its former American aspect.

Among the old time aristocracy bearing Knickerbocker names there are a few colored people who delight in talking of the fine families and past wealth of old Greenwich Village. Scornful of the gibberish-speaking Italians, they sigh, too, at their own race as they see it, for the ambitious Negro has moved uptown, leaving this section largely to widowed and deserted women and degenerates. The once handsome houses, altered to accommodate many families, are rotten and unwholesome, while the newer tenements of West Third Street are darkened by the elevated road, and shelter vice that knows no race. Altogether, this is not a neighborhood to attract the newcomer. Here alone in New York I have found the majority of the adults northern born, men and women who, unsuccessful in their struggle with city life, have been left behind in these old forgotten streets.

The second section, north of the first, lies between West Fourteenth and West Fifty-ninth streets, and Sixth Avenue and the Hudson River. In 1880 this was the center of the Negro population, but business has entered some of the streets, the Pennsylvania Railroad has scooped out acres for its terminal, and while the colored houses do not diminish in number, they show no decided increase. No one street is given over to the Negro, but a row of two or three or six or even eight tenements shelters the black man. The shelter afforded is poorer than that given the white resident whose dwelling touches the black, the rents are a little higher, and the landlord fails to pay attention to ragged paper, or to a ceiling which scatters plaster flakes upon the floor. In the Thirties there are rear tenements reached by narrow alleyways. Crimes are committed by black neighbor against black neighbor, and the entrance to the rear yard offers a tempting place for a girl to linger at night. A rear tenement is New York's only approach to the alley of cities farther south.

There are startling and happy surprises in all tenement neighborhoods, and I recall turning one afternoon from a dark yard into a large beautiful room. Muslin curtains concealed the windows, the brass bed was covered with a thick white counterpane, and on either side of the fireplace, where coal burned brightly

PLACE OF BIRTH OF 1036 NEW YORK NEGRO TENEMENT DWELLERS

	Totals	East Side	Greenwich Village	Middle West Side	San Juan Hill	Upper West Side
New England	18	1	4	7	5	1
West	11	1	0	5	4	1
New York	157	6	47	42	55	7
New Jersey	18	1	4	3	9	1
Pennsylvania	19	0	3	3	12	1
Maryland	37	1	0	6	27	3
District of Columbia	26	0	1	5	16	4
Virginia	375	8	15	71	244	37
Carolinas	217	6	16	64	127	4
Gulf States	65	0	2	23	39	1
Canada	2	0	0	1	0	0
West Indies	87	1	6	13	67	0
Europe	4	0	1	0	3	0
	1036	25	100	243	608	60

Note: These figures were obtained chiefly from personal visits.

in an open grate, were two rare engravings. It was a workroom, and the mistress of the house, steady, capable, and very black, was at her ironing board. By her sat the colored mammy of the story book rocking lazily in her chair. She explained to me that her daughter had found her down South, two years ago, and brought her to this northern home, where she had nothing to do, for her daughter could make fifty dollars a month. This home picture was made lastingly memorable by the younger woman's telling me softly as she went with me to the door, "I was sold from my mother, down in Georgia, when I was two years old.

I ain't sure she's my mother. *She* thinks so; but I can't ever be sure."

Homes beautiful both in appearance and in spirit can rarely occur where people must dwell in great poverty, but there are many efforts at attractive family life on these streets. A few of the blocks are orderly and quiet. Thirty-seventh Street, between Eighth and Ninth avenues, is largely given over to the colored and is rough and noisy. Here and down by the river at Hell's Kitchen the rioting in 1900 between the Irish and the Negro took place. Men are ready for a fight today, and the children see much of hard drinking and quick blows.

"The poorer the family, the lower is the quarter in which it must live, and the more enviable appears the fortune of the anti-social class." [3] A vicious world dwells in these streets and makes notorious this section of New York. For this is a part of the Tenderloin district, and at night, after the children's cries have ceased, and the fathers and mothers who have worked hard during the day have put out their lights, the automobiles rush swiftly past, bearing the men of the "superior race." Temptation is continuous, and the child that grows up pure in thought and deed does so in spite of his surroundings.

Before reaching West Fifty-ninth Street, the beginning of our third district, we come upon a Negro block at West Fifty-third Street. When years ago the elevated railroad was erected on this fashionable street, white people began to sell out and rent to Negroes; and today you find here three colored hotels, the colored Young Men's and Young Women's Christian Associations, the offices of many colored doctors and lawyers, and three large beautiful colored churches. The din of the elevated drowns alike the doctor's voice and his patient's, the client's and the preacher's.

From Fifty-ninth Street, walking north on Tenth Avenue, we begin to ascend a hill that grows in steepness until we reach Sixty-second Street. The avenue is lined with small stores kept

3. S. N. Patten, *New Basis of Civilization,* p. 52.

by Italians and Germans, but to the left the streets, sloping rapidly to the Hudson River, are filled with tenements, huge double-deckers, built to within ten feet of the rear of the twenty-five foot lot, accommodating four families on each of the five floors. We can count four hundred and seventy-nine homes on one side of the street alone!

This is our third district, San Juan Hill, so called by an onlooker who saw the policemen charging up during one of the once common race fights. It is a bit of Africa, as Negroid in aspect as any district you are likely to visit in the South. A large majority of its residents are Southerners and West Indians, and it presents an interesting study of the Negro poor in a large northern city. The block on Sixtieth Street has some white residents, but the blocks on Sixty-first, Sixty-second, and Sixty-third are given over entirely to colored. On the square made by the north side of Sixty-first, the south side of Sixty-second, and Tenth and West End avenues, 5.4 acres, the state census of 1905 showed 6173 inhabitants.[4] All but a few of these must have been Negroes, as the avenue sides of the block, occupied by whites, are short and with low houses. It is the long line of five-story tenements, running eight hundred feet down the two streets, that brings up the enumeration. The dwellings on Sixty-first and Sixty-second streets are human hives, honeycombed with little rooms thick with human beings. Bedrooms open into air shafts that admit no fresh breezes, only foul air carrying too often the germs of disease.

The people on the hill are known for their rough behavior, their readiness to fight, their coarse talk. Vice is abroad, not in insidious form as in the more well-to-do neighborhood farther north, but open and cheap. Boys play at craps unmolested,

4. Some doubt is cast upon this figure. The New York Health Department in an enumeration of its own, in 1905, found a population of 3833. There is no question, however, of the great congestion of this block and the one north and south of it. The erection of new tenements has gone on rapidly since 1905, sweeping away the children's playgrounds, and making this one of the most crowded centers of New York.

gambling is prevalent, and Negro loafers hang about the street corners and largely support the Tenth Avenue saloons.

But San Juan Hill has many respectable families, and within the past five years it has taken a decided turn for the better. The improvement has been chiefly upon Sixty-third Street where two model tenements, one holding one hundred, the other one hundred and sixty-one families, have been opened under the management of the City and Suburban Homes Company, the larger one having been erected by Mr. Henry Phipps. Planning for a 4 per cent return on their investment, these landlords have rented only to respectable families, and their rule has changed the character of the block.[5] Old houses have been remodeled to compete with the newer dwellings, street rows have ceased, and the police captain of the district, we are told, now counts this as one of the peaceful and law-abiding blocks of the city. When its other blocks show a like improvement, San Juan Hill will no longer merit its belligerent name.

The lower East Side of Manhattan, a many-storied mass of tenements and workshops, where immigrants labor and sleep in their tiny crowded rooms, was once a fashionable American district. At that time Negroes dwelt near the whites as barbers, caterers, and coachmen, as laundresses and waiting maids. But with the removal of the people whom they served, the colored men and women left also, and it is difficult to find an African face among the hundreds of thousands of Europeans south of Fourteenth Street. On Pell Street, in the Chinese quarter, there used to be two colored families on friendly terms with their

5. Too much cannot be said of the beneficial effect of good housing in a colored neighborhood, when under such able management as the City and Suburban Homes Company. Decent homes under competent management are absolutely necessary to an improvement in the Negro quarters of Manhattan and of Brooklyn as well. I can speak with some authority of the good done by the Phipps houses on West Sixty-third Street, as I lived, for eight months, the only white tenant in the 161 apartments. Church and philanthropy had done and are doing excellent work on these blocks, but a sudden and marked improvement came from good housing, from the building of clean, healthful homes for law-abiding people.

neighbors, who, however, went uptown for their pleasures and their church.

It is not until we reach Third Avenue and Forty-third Street that we come to the East Side Negro tenement. From this point, such houses run, a straggling line, chiefly between Second and Third avenues, to the Bronx where the more well-to-do among the colored live. At Ninety-seventh Street, and on up to One Hundredth Street, dark faces are numerous. About six hundred and fifty Negro families live on these four streets and around the corner on Third Avenue. Occasionally they live in houses occupied by Jews or Italians. Above this section there are a number of Negro tenements in the One Hundred and Thirties, between Madison and Fifth avenues—almost a West Side neighborhood, since it adjoins the large colored quarter to the west of Fifth Avenue. On the whole, the East Side is not often sought by the colored as a place of residence. Their important churches are in another part of the city, and every New Yorker knows the difficulty in making a way across Central Park. Yet, the neighborhood is not uncivil to them, and one rarely reads here of race friction. Doubtless this is in part owing to the smallness of the population, all of Manhattan east of Fifth Avenue containing but 14 per cent of the apartments occupied by colored in the city; but it is partly, too, that Jews and Italians prove less belligerent tenement neighbors than Irish.

Five years ago, those of us who were interested in the Negro poor continually heard of their difficulty in securing a place to live. Not only were they unable to rent in neighborhoods suitable for respectable men and women, but dispossession, caused perhaps by the inroad of business, meant a despairing hunt for any home at all. People clung to miserable dwellings, where no improvements had been made for years, thankful to have a roof to shelter them. Yet all the time new-law tenements were being built, and Gentile and Jew were leaving their former apartments in haste to get into these more attractive dwellings. At length the Negro got his chance; not a very good one, but something better than New York had yet offered him—a chance to follow

into the houses left vacant by the white tenents. Owing in part
to the energy of Negro real-estate agents, in part to rapid building operations, desirable streets, near the subway and the elevated
railroad, were thrown open to the colored. This Negro quarter,
the last we have to note and the newest, has been created in
the past eight years. When the Tenement House Department
tabulated the 1900 census figures for the Borough of Manhattan,
and showed the nationalities and races on each block, it found
only 300 colored families in a neighborhood that today accom-
modates 4473 colored families.[6] This large increase is on six
streets, West Ninety-ninth, between Eighth and Ninth avenues,
West One Hundred and Nineteenth, between Seventh and Eighth
avenues, and West One Hundred and Thirty-third to One Hundred and Thirty-sixth streets, between Fifth and Seventh avenues,
with a few houses between Seventh and Eighth, and on Lenox
Avenue. There are colored tenements north and south of this;
and while these figures are correct today,[7] they may be wrong
tomorrow, for new tenements are continually given over to the
Negro people. Moreover, on all of these streets are colored
boarding and lodging houses, crowded with humanity. Houses
today fall into the hands of the Negro as a child's blocks, placed
on end, tumble when a push is given to the first in the line. *The
New York Times,* in August, 1905, gives a graphic account of
the entrance of the colored tenant on West Ninety-ninth Street.
Two houses had been opened for a short time to Negroes when
the other house owners capitulated, and the colored influx came:
"The street was so choked with vehicles Saturday that some of
the drivers had to wait with their teams around the corners for
an opportunity to get into it. A constant stream of furniture
trucks loaded with the household effects of a new colony of
colored people who are invading the choice locality is pouring
into the street. Another equally long procession, moving in the

6. The Tenement House Department tabulated the number of Negro
families living in tenements on these streets. I have counted the number
of flats rented to colored people.

7. July 15, 1910.

other direction, is carrying away the household goods of the whites from their homes of years." The movement is not always so swift as this, but it is continuous.

This last colored neighborhood perhaps ought not to be spoken of as belonging to the poor; not to Lanier's poor whose door pressed so tighteningly inward. Here are homes where it is possible, with sufficient money, to live in privacy, and with the comforts of steam heat and a private bath. But rents are high, and if money is scarce, the apartment must be crowded and privacy lost. Moreover, vice has made its way into these newly acquired streets. The sporting class will always pay more and demand fewer improvements than the workers, and, unable to protect himself, the respectable tenant finds his children forced to live in close propinquity to viciousness. Each of these new streets has this objectionable element in its population, for while some agents make earnest efforts to keep the property they handle respectable, they find the owner wants money more than respectability.

In our walk up and down Manhattan, turning aside and searching for Negro-tenanted streets, we ought to see one thing with clearness—that the majority of the colored population live on a comparatively few blocks. This is a new and important feature of their New York life, and in certain parts of the city it develops a color problem, for while you seem an inappreciable quantity when you constitute 2 per cent of the population in the borough, you are of importance when you form 100 per cent of the population of your street. This congestion is accompanied by a segregation of the race. The dwellers in these tenements are largely newcomers, men and women from the South and the West Indies,[8] seeking the North for greater freedom and for economic opportunity. Like any other strangers they are glad to

8. The yearly arrivals of "African blacks" at the port of New York, secured from the Immigration Commissioner, are as follows: 1902–1903, 110; 1903–1904, 547; 1904–1905, 1189; 1905–1906, 1757; 1906–1907, 2054; 1907–1908, 1820; 1908–1909, 2119. The year runs from July 1 to June 30.

make their home among familiar faces, and they settle in the already crowded places on the West Side. Freedom to live on the East Side next door to a Bohemian family may be very well, but sociability is better. The housewife who timidly hangs her clothes on the roof her first Monday morning in New York is pleased to find the next line swinging with the laundry of a Richmond acquaintance, who instructs her in the perplexing housekeeping devices of her flat. No chattering foreigner could do that. And while to be welcome in a white church is inspiring, to find the girl you knew at home, in the pew next to you, is still more delightful when you have arrived, tired and homesick, at the great city of New York. So the colored working people, like the Italians and Jews and other nationalities, have their quarter in which they live very much by themselves, paying little attention to their white neighbors. If the white people of the city have forced this upon them, they have easily accepted it. Should this 2 per cent of the population be compelled to distribute itself mathematically over the city, each ward and street having its correct quota, it would evince dissatisfaction. This is not true of the well-to-do element, but of the mass of the Negro workers whose homes we have been visiting. Loving sociability, these newcomers to the city—and it is in the most segregated districts that the greater number of southern and British born Negroes are found—keep to their own streets and live to themselves. If they occupy all the sidewalk as they talk over important matters in front of their church, the outsider passing should recognize that he is an intruder and take to the curb. He would leave the sidewalk entirely, were he on Hester Street or Mulberry Bend. Newcomers to New York usually segregate, and the Negro is no exception.

While congestion and segregation seem important to us as we look at these colored quarters, I suspect that the matter most pertinent to the Negro newcomer is, not where he will live nor how he will live, but whether he will be able to live in New York at all, whether he can meet the landlord's agent the day he comes to the door. For New York rents have mounted upwards as

have her tenements. The Phipps model houses, built especially
to benefit the poor, charge twenty-five dollars a month for four
tiny rooms and bath; and while this is a little more than the dark
old-time rooms would bring, it takes about all of the twenty-five
dollars you make running an elevator, to get a flat in New York.
What wonder that, once secured, it is overrun with lodgers, or
that, if privacy is maintained, there is not enough money left to
feed and clothe the growing household. The once familiar song
of the colored comedian still rings true in New York:

> Rufus Rastus Johnson Brown,
> What you gwine ter do when de rent comes roun'?

CHAPTER THREE

The Child of
the Tenement

WITHIN THE LAST FEW YEARS white Americans, many of whom were formerly ignorant of their condition, have been taught that they are possessed of a racial antipathy for human beings whose color is not their own. They have a "natural contrariety," "a dislike that seems constitutional" toward the dark tint that they see on another's face. But however well they may have conned their lesson, it breaks down or is likely to be forgotten in the presence of a Negro baby; for a healthy colored baby is a subject, not for natural contrariety, but for sympathetic cuddling. They are most engaging newcomers, these "delicate bronze statuettes," [1] only warm with life, and smiling good will upon their world.

Not many colored babies are born in New York, at least not enough to keep pace with the deaths. The year 1908 saw in all the boroughs 1973 births as against 2212 deaths at all ages. [2]

In this same year the colored births for Manhattan and the Bronx were 1459, and the deaths under one year of age 424, an infant mortality rate of 290 to every thousand. [3] That is, two

1. Dudley Kidd, *Savage Childhood,* a delightful book.
2. Report of the Department of Health, City of New York, 1908, pp. 844, 849. The returns for births, the report states, are incomplete.
3. This per cent is obtained from two sources, the births from the

29

babies in every seven died under one year of age. The white infant mortality rate was 127.7, a little less than half that of the colored.

Why should we have in New York this enormous colored infant death rate? Many physicians believe it indicates a lack of physical stamina in the Negro, an inability to resist disease. This may be so, but before falling back upon race as an explanation of high infant mortality, we need to exhaust other possible causes. We do not question the vitality of the white race when we read that in parts of Russia 500 babies out of every thousand die within the year; nor do we believe the people of Fall River, a factory town in Massachusetts, have an inherent inability to resist disease, though their infant mortality rate in 1900 was 260 in one thousand births. We look in these latter cases, as we should in the former, to see if we find those conditions which careful students of the subject tell us accompany a high infant death rate.

Among the first of the accepted causes of infant mortality is the overcrowding of cities. We have viewed overcrowding as a usual condition among the Negroes of New York, and have seen the small, ill-ventilated bedroom where the baby spends much of its life. Heat, with its accompanying growth of bacteria and swift process of decomposition, is a second cause. New York's high infant mortality comes in the summer months when in the poorest quarters it has been known to reach four hundred in the thousand.[4] In the hot, crowded tenements, and no place can be so hot as New York in one of its July record-breaking weeks, the babies die like flies, and yet not like flies, for the flies buzz in hundreds about the little hot faces. Excitement, late hours, constant restlessness, these, too, cause infant mortality. On a city block tenanted by hundreds of men and women and little children, no hour of the night is free from some disturbance. Children whimper as they wake from the heat, babies cry shrilly, and the brightly lighted streets are rarely without the sound of

Department of Health report, and the deaths from the Mortality Statistics of the United States Census, 1908. "Colored" includes Chinese, a negligible quantity in the infant population.

4. Third Annual Report of the New York Milk Committee, 1909.

human footsteps. The sensitive newborn organism knows nothing of the quiet and restful darkness of nature's night.

But the most important cause of infant mortality[5] is improper infant feeding. And here we meet with a condition that confronts the Negro babies of New York far more than it confronts the white. For a properly fed baby is a breast-fed baby, or else one whose food has been prepared with great care, and mothers forced by necessity to go out to work, cannot themselves give their babies this proper food. It is among the infants of mothers at work that mortality is high. Mr. G. Newman, an English authority on this subject, gives an interesting example of this in Lancashire, where, during the American Civil War, many of the cotton operatives were out of employment and many more worked only half time. Privation was great. A quarter of the mill hands were in receipt of poor relief, the general death rate increased, but *the infant mortality rate decreased*. The mothers, forced by circumstances to remain away from the factory, though in a state of semistarvation, by their nursing and by their care of the home preserved the lives of their infants. Negro mothers, owing to the low wage earned by their husbands, for the general welfare of the family and to avoid semistarvation, like the Lancashire women, leave their homes, but they thereby sacrifice the lives of many of their babies. The percentage for 1900 of Negro married women in New York engaging in self-supporting work was 31.4 in every hundred; of white married women 4.2 in every hundred, seven times as many in proportion among the Negroes as among the whites.[6] The Negro also shows a large percentage of widows, a quarter of all the female population over ten years of age. Some of these, we have no means of knowing how many, are widows only in name, and have babies for whom they must in some way provide support. The colored mother who has no husband often takes a position in domestic service and boards her baby, paying usually by the month, and finding the opportunity to visit her infant perhaps once a week. Sometimes she

5. See G. Newman, *Infant Mortality*, for a careful study of this whole subject.
6. Census, 1900, combination of Population table and Women at Work.

secures a "baby tender" who can give kindly, intelligent care; but under the best conditions her child will be bottle-fed and in tenement surroundings inimical to health, while sometimes the woman to whom she intrusts her infant will be ignorant of the simplest matters of hygiene.

I remember an old colored woman, she must be dead by this time, who kept a baby farm. Her health was poor, and when I saw her, she had taken to her bed and lay in a dark room with two infants at her side. They were indescribably puny, with sunken cheeks and skinny arms and hands, weighing what a normal child should weigh at birth, and yet six and seven months old. The woman talked to me enthusiastically of salvation and gave filthy bottles to her charges. She was exceptionally incompetent, but there are others doing her work, too old or too ignorant properly to attend to the babies under their care.

Mothers who go out to day's work are also unable to nurse their babies or to prepare all their food. The infant is placed in the care of some neighbor or of a growing daughter, who may be the impatient "little mother" of a number of charges. When the hot summer comes, such a baby is likely to fall the victim of epidemic diarrhea, caused by pollution of the milk. Newman has a striking chart of infant death rates in Paris in which he pictures a rate mounting in one week as high as 256 in the thousand among the artificially fed infants, while for the same week, among the breast-fed babies, the mortality is 32. The Negro mother, seeking self-support by keeping clean another's house or caring for another's children, finds her own offspring swiftly taken from her by a disease that only her nourishing care could forestall.[7]

Remedial measures have for some time been taken in New York to check infant mortality, and they have met with some success. The distribution of pasturized milk by Mr. Nathan Straus, the establishment of milk stations during the summer months in New York and Brooklyn where mothers at slight cost

---

7. It is interesting to see that the married women of Fall River, where we found a very high infant death rate, show a percentage of married women at work of twenty in a hundred.

may secure proper infant food, and where much educative work is done by the visiting nurse, the multiplication of day nurseries, all these have helped to decrease the death rate. The Negroes have been benefited by these remedial agencies, but their percentage of 290 is still a matter for grave attention.

Two out of seven of New York's Negro babies die in the first year, but the other five grow up, some with puny arms and rickety legs, others again too hardy for bad food or bad air to harm.

Like the babies these children suffer from their mother's absence at work. Family ties are loose, and more than other children they are handicapped by lack of proper home care. In an examination of the records of the Children's Court for three years I found that out of 717 arraignments of colored children, 221 were for improper guardianship, 30.8 per cent of the whole. Among the Russian children of the East Side, Tenth and Eleventh wards, only 15 per cent of arraignments were on this complaint, indicating twice as many children without parental care among the colored as among the children of the Tenth and Eleventh wards. Rough colored girls, also, whose habits were too depraved to permit of their remaining without restraint, were frequently committed to reformatories.

Truancy is not uncommon in colored neighborhoods, though few cases come before the courts. Sometimes the boy or girl is kept at home to care for the younger children, but again, lacking the mother's oversight, he remains on the street when he should be in school, or arrives late with ill-prepared lessons.

Asking a teacher of long experience among colored and white children concerning their respective scholarship, he assured me that the colored child could do as well as the white, but didn't. "From 20 to 50 per cent of the mothers of my colored children," he said, "go out to work. There is no one to oversee the child's tasks, and consequently little conscientious study."

One can scarcely blame the children; and certainly one cannot blame the mothers for toiling for their support. And the fathers, though they work faithfully, are rarely able to earn enough unaided to support their families. Perhaps in time the city may improve matters by opening its schoolrooms for a study period in the afternoon.

But meanwhile the children are without proper care. This is not hard to endure in the summer, but in winter it is very trying to be without a home. Poor little cold boys and girls, some of them mere babies! You see them in the late afternoon sitting on the tenement stairs, waiting for the long day to be done. It seems a week since they were inside eating their breakfast. The city has not pauperized them with a luncheon, and they have had only cold food since morning. Sometimes they have been all day without nourishment. When the door is opened at last, there are many helpful things for them to do for their mother, and reading and arithmetic are relegated to so late an hour that their problem is only temporarily solved by sleep.

Not all the colored working women, however, go out for employment. Laundry work is an important home industry, and one may watch many mothers at their tubs or ironing boards from Monday morning until Saturday night. This makes the tenement rooms, tiny enough at best, sadly cluttered, but it does not deprive the children of the presence of their mother, who accepts a smaller income to remain at home with them. For after we have made full allowance for the lessening of family ties among the Negroes by social and economic pressure, we find that the majority of the colored boys and girls receive a due share of proper parental oversight. They are fed on appetizing food, cleanly and prettily dressed, they are encouraged to study and to improve their position, and they are given all the advantages that it is possible for their mothers and fathers to secure.

Jack London tells in the "Children of the Abyss" of the East Side of London, where "they have dens and lairs into which to crawl for sleeping purposes, and that is all. One can not travesty the word by calling such dens and lairs 'homes.' " I have seen thousands of Negro dwelling places, but I cannot think of half a dozen, however great their poverty, where this description would be correct. No matter how dingy the tenement, or how long the hours of work, the mother, and the father, too, try to make the "four walls and a ceiling" to which they return, home.

Visitors among the New York poor, in the past and in the present, testify that given the same income or lack of income, the colored do not allow their surroundings to become so cheerless or so filthy as the white, and that when there is an opportunity for the mother to spend some time in the house, the rooms take on an air of pleasant refinement. Pictures decorate the walls, the sideboard contains many pretty dishes, and the table is set three times a day. Meals are not eaten out of the paper bag common on New York's East Side, but there is something of formality about the dinner, and good table manners are taught the children. The tenement dwelling becomes a home, and the boys and girls pass a happy childhood in it.

Watching the colored children for many months in their play and work, I have looked for possible distinctive traits. The second generation of New Yorkers greatly resembles the "Young America" of all nationalities of the city, shrill-voiced, disrespectful, easily diverted, whether at work or at play, shrewd, alert, and mischievous—the New York street child. I remember once helping with a club of eight boys where seven nationalities were represented, and where no one could have distinguished Irish from German or Jew from Italian, with his eyes shut. Had a Negro been brought up among them he would quickly have taken on their ways. Of the colored children who model their lives after their mischievous young white neighbors, many outdo the whites in depravity and lawlessness; but among the boys and girls who live by themselves, as on San Juan Hill, one sees occasional interesting traits.

The records of the Children's Court of New York (Boroughs of Manhattan and the Bronx) throw a little light on this matter, and are sufficiently important to quote with some fullness. For the three years studied, 1904, 1905, 1906, I tabulated the cases of the colored children brought before the court, and also the cases of the children of the Tenth and Eleventh wards, chiefly Hungarians and Russian Jews, expecting to find, in two such dissimilar groups, interesting comparisons. The following table shows the result of this study. The court in its annual report gives the figures for the total number of arrests which I have incorporated in my table:

RECORD OF ARRESTS IN CHILDREN'S COURT OF MANHATTAN
AND THE BRONX FOR 1904, 1905, 1906

	Negro arrests		10th and 11th wards arrests		Total arrests for all children in Manhattan and Bronx	
	No. of children	Arrests per cent	No. of children	Arrests per cent	No. of children	Arrests per cent
Petit larceny	56	7.8	139	6.8	2,697	10.1
Grand larceny	27	3.8	108	5.3	878	3.3
Burglary—Robbery	27	3.8	116	5.7	1,383	5.2
Assault	27	3.8	61	3.0	669	2.5
Improper guardianship	221	30.8	305	15.0	6,386	23.9
Disorderly child—ungovernable child	90	12.6	124	6.1	1,980	7.4
Depraved girl	33	4.6	21	1.1	312	1.2
Violation of labor law	0	0	73	3.5	592	2.1
Unlicensed peddling[1]	0	0	130	6.4	0	.0
Truancy	5	.7	23	1.0	298	1.1
Malicious mischief	1	.1	9	.4	179	.7
Violation of Park Corporation ordinances	0	0	25	1.2	175	.7
Mischief, including craps, throwing stones, building bonfires, fighting, etc.	214	29.8	896	43.7	10,267	38.4
Unclassified felonies, misdemeanors	13	1.8	16	.7	799	3.0
All others	3	.4	3	.1	90	.4
	717	100.0	2049	100.0	26,705	100.0

Percentage of Negro to total, 1904–1907	2.7
Percentage of Negro to total, 1907–1910	1.9

1. My tabulations of the Negro and Tenth- and Eleventh-ward children are from the Court's unpublished records to which I was allowed access. The absence of any figures for unlicensed peddling in the total indicates that in its printed reports the Court has included unlicensed peddling with unclassified misdemeanors.

Our table shows us that which we have already noted, the high percentage of improper guardianship among the Negroes and the grave number of depraved Negro girls. For the sins of petit larceny, grand larceny, and burglary, putting the three together, the colored child shows a slightly smaller percentage than the East Side white, a noticeably smaller percentage than the total number of children. The sin of theft is often swiftly attributed to a black face, but this percentage indicates that the colored child has no "innate tendency" to steal. Ten per cent of the arrests among the East Side children are for unlicensed peddling and violation of the labor law, but no little Negro boys plunge into the business world before their time. They have no keen commercial sense to lead them to undertake transactions on their own account, and they are not desired by purchasers of boy labor in the city.

The most important heading, numerically, is that of mischief, and here the Negro falls far behind the Eastsider, behind the average for the whole. While depravity among the girls and improper guardianship are the race's most serious defects, as shown by the arrests among its children in New York, tractability and a decent regard for law are among its merits. The colored child, especially if he is in a segregated neighborhood, is not greatly inclined to mischief. My own experience has shown me that life in a tenement on San Juan Hill is devoid of the ingenious, exasperating deviltry of an Irish or German-American neighborhood. No daily summons calls one to the door only to hear wildly scurrying footsteps on the stairs. Mailboxes are left solely for the postman's use, and hallways are not defaced by obscene writing. There is plenty of crap shooting, rarely interfered with by the police, but there is little impertinent annoyance or destructiveness.

An observer, watching the little colored boys and girls as they play on the city streets, finds much that is attractive and pleasant. They sing their songs, learned at school and on the playground, fly their kites, spin their tops, run their races. They usually finish what they begin, not turning at the first interruption to take up something else. They move more deliberately than most children, and their voices are slower to adopt the New York screech than those of their Irish neighbors on the block above them. Altogether they are attractive children, particularly the smaller ones, who are more energetic than their big brothers and sisters. Good manners are often evident. While receiving an afternoon call from two girls, aged four and five, I was invited by the older to partake of half a peanut, the other half of which she split in two and generously shared with her companion. "Gim' me five cents," I once heard a Negro boy of twelve say to his mother who walked past him on the street. She did not seem to hear, but the boy's companion, a youth of the same age, reproved him severely for his rude speech. When walking with an Irish friend, who had worked among the children of her own race, I saw a colored boy run swiftly up the block to meet his mother. He kissed her, took her bundle from her, and carrying it under his arm, walked quietly by her side to their home. "There are many boys here," I said, "who are just as courteous as that." "Is that so?" she retorted quickly. "Then you needn't be explaining to me any further the reason for the high death rate."

The gentle, chivalrous affection of the child for its mother is daily to be seen among these boys and girls. "Your African," said Mary Kingsley, "is little better than a slave to his mother, whom he loves with a love he gives to none other. This love of his mother is so dominant a factor in his life that it must be taken into consideration in attempting to understand the true Negro." [8] And if the child lavishes affection upon its parent, the mother in turn gives untiringly to her child. She is the "mammy" of whom we have so often heard, but with her loving care bestowed, as it should be, upon her own offspring. She tries to keep her child clean in body and spirit and to train it to be gentle and good; and in return usually she receives a stanch devotion. I once found fault with a colored girl of ten years for her rude behavior with her girl companions, adding that perhaps she did

8. Mary Kingsley, *West African Studies,* p. 319.

not know any better, at which she turned on me almost fiercely and said, "It's our fault; we know better. Our mothers learn us. It's we that's bold." As one watches the boys and girls walking quietly up the street of a Sunday afternoon to their Sunday school, neatly and cleanly dressed, one appreciates the anxious, maternal care that strives as best it knows how, to rear honest and God-fearing men and women.

Paul Lawrence Dunbar has painted the Negro father, his "little brown baby wif sparklin' eyes," nestling close in his arms. Working at unusual hours, the colored man often has a part of the day to give to his family, and one sees him wheeling the baby in its carriage, or playing with the older boys and girls.

Negroes seem naturally a gentle, loving people. As you live with them and watch them in their homes, you find some coarseness, but little real brutality. Rarely does a father or mother strike a child. Travelers in Central and West Africa describe them as the most friendly of savage folk, and where, as in our city, they live largely to themselves, they keep something of these characteristics. But it is only a step in New York from Africa into Italy or Ireland; and the step may bring a sad jostling to native friendliness. To hold his own with his white companions on the street or in school, the Negro must become pugnacious, callous to insult, ready to hit back when affronted. Many are like the little girl who told me that she did not care to play with white children, "because," she explained, "my mother tells me to smack any one who calls me nigger, and I ain't looking for trouble." The colored children aren't looking for trouble. They have a tendency to run away from it if they see it in the form of a gang of boys coming to them around the corner. They believe if they had a fight, it wouldn't be a fair one, and that if the policeman came, he would arrest them and not their Irish enemies. So they grow up on streets through which few white men pass, leading their own lives with their own people and thinking not overmuch of the other race that surrounds them. But the day comes when school is over, and the outside world, however indifferent they may be to it, must be met. They must go out and grapple with it for the means to hire a cooking stove and a dark bedroom of their own; they must think of making money. So they stand at the corner of their street, looking out, and then move slowly on to find what opportunity is theirs to come to a full manhood. The way ahead does not seem very bright, and some move so timidly that failure is sure to meet them at the first turning. But some have the courage of the little colored girl, aged four, who led a line of kindergarten children up their street and then on to the unknown country that lay between them and Central Park. At the first block a mob of Irish boys fell upon them, running between the lines, throwing sticks, and calling "nigger" with screams and jeers. The leader held her head high, paying no attention to her persecutors. She neither quickened nor slowed her pace, and when the child at her side fell back, she pulled her hand and said, "Don't notice them. Walk straight ahead."

CHAPTER FOUR

Earning a Living—
Manual Labor
and the Trades

IN *The American Race Problem,* one of our recent important books upon the Negro, the author, Mr. Alfred Holt Stone of Mississippi, after a survey of the world, declares that "to me, it seems the plainest fact confronting the Negro is that there is but one area of any size wherein his race may obey the command to eat its bread in the sweat of its face side by side with the white man. That area is composed of the Southern United States." [1]

On examination we find that only men of English and North European stock are "white" to Mr. Stone, and that his statement is too sweeping by a continent or two, but as applying to the United States, it will usually meet with unqualified approval. It is generally believed that discrimination continually retards the Negro in his search for employment in the North, while in the South "he is given a man's chance in the commercial world." Northern men visiting southern colored industrial schools advise the pupils to remain where they are, and restless spirits among

1. Alfred Holt Stone, *Studies in the American Race Problem,* p. 164.

the race are assured that it is better to submit to some personal oppression than to go to a land of uncertain employment. The past glory of the North is dwelt upon, its days of black waiters, and barbers, and coachmen, but the present is painted in harsh colors.

There is some truth in this comparison of economic conditions among the Negroes in the North and in the South, but it must not be taken too literally. Today's tendency to minimize southern and maximize northern race difficulties, while strengthening the bonds between white Americans, sometimes obscures the real issues regarding colored labor in this country. We need to look carefully at conditions in numbers of selected localities, and we can find no northern city more worthy of our study than New York.

The New York Negro constitutes today but 2 per cent of the population of Manhattan, 1.8 per cent of that of Greater New York; and, as many workers in Manhattan live in Brooklyn, the larger area is the better one to consider. In 1900, the census volume on occupations gives the number of males over ten years of age engaged in gainful occupations in Greater New York at 1,102,471, and of that number 20,395 or 1.8 per cent, eighteen in every thousand, are Negroes. In Atlanta, to take a southern commercial center, 351 out of every thousand male workers are Negroes. This enormous difference in the proportion of colored workers to white must never be forgotten in considering the labor situation North and South. We cannot expect in the North to see the Negro monopolizing an industry which demands a larger share of workers than he can produce, nor need we admit that he has lost an occupation when he does not control it.

We often come upon such a statement as that of Samuel R. Scottron, a colored businessman, who, writing in 1905, said, "The Italian, Sicilian, Greek, occupy quite every industry that was confessedly the Negro's forty years ago. They have the boot-black stands, the news stands, barbers' shops, waiters' situations, restaurants, janitorships, catering business, stevedoring, steam-

boat work, and other situations occupied by Negroes." [2] Did the
colored men have all this forty years ago when they were only
1.5 per cent of the population? If so, there were giants in those
days, or New York was much simpler in its habits than now.
At present the control by the colored people of any such an array
of industries would be quite impossible. To take four out of the
nine occupations enumerated: the census of 1900 gives the
number of waiters at 31,211; barbers, 12,022; janitors, 6184;
bootblacks, 2648; a total of 52,065. But in 1900 there were only
20,395 Negro males engaged in gainful occupations in New
York. Without a vigorous astral body the 20,000-odd colored
men could not occupy half these jobs. If they dominated in the
field of waiters they must abandon handling the razor, and not
all the colored boys could muster 2684 strong to black the boots
of Greater New York. We must at the outset recognize that as
a labor factor the Negro in New York is insignificant.

The volume of the federal census for 1900 on occupations
shows us how the Negroes are employed in New York City.
There are five occupational divisions, and the Negroes and
whites are divided among them as follows:

	White	Per cent	Negro	Per cent
Agricultural pursuits	9,853	.9	251	1.2
Professional service	60,037	5.6	729	3.6
Domestic and personal service	189,282	17.6	11,843	58.1
Trade and transportation	398,997	37.1	5,798	28.4
Manufacturing and mechanical pursuits	417,634	38.8	1,774	8.7
Total	1,075,803	100.0	20,395	100.0

But in examining in detail the occupations under these different
headings, we get a clearer view of the place the Negro maintains

2. New York *Age,* August 24, 1905.

as a laborer by finding out how many workers he supplies to every thousand workers in a given occupation. He should average eighteen if he is to occupy the same economic status as the white man. Taking the first (numerically) important division, domestic and personal service, we get the following table:

DOMESTIC AND PERSONAL SERVICE

	Total number of males in each occupation	Number of Negroes in each occupation	Number of Negroes to each 1000 workers in occupation
Barbers and hairdressers	12,022	215	18
Bootblacks	2,648	51	20
Launderers	6,881	70	10
Servants and waiters	31,211	6,280	201
Stewards	1,366	140	103
Nurses	1,342	22	16
Boarding and lodging housekeepers	474	10	21
Hotel keepers	3,139	23	7
Restaurant keepers	2,869	116	40
Saloon keepers and bartenders	17,656	111	6
Janitors and sextons	6,184	800	129
Watchmen, firemen, policemen	16,093	116	7
Soldiers, sailors, marines	3,707	56	15
Laborers (including elevator tenders, laborers in coal yards, longshoremen, and stevedores)	98,531	3,719	38
Total, including some occupations not specified	206,215	11,843	57

The most important of these groups, not only in absolute numbers, but in proportion to the whole working population, is the servants and waiters. Two hundred out of every thousand (we must remember that the proportion to the population would be eighteen out of every thousand) are holding positions with which they have long been identified in America. We cannot tell from the census how many "live out," or how many are able to go nightly to their homes, how many have good jobs, and how many are in second- and third-rate places. A study of my own of 716 colored men helps to answer one of these questions. Out of 176 men coming under the servants' and waiters' classification, I found 5 caterers, 24 cooks, 26 butlers, 30 general utility men, 41 hotel men, and 50 waiters. Sixty per cent of the 176 lived in their own homes, not in their masters'. Some of the cooks and waiters were on Pullman trains or on river boats or steamers; only a few were in first-class positions in New York. In the summer many of these men are likely to go to country hotels, and with the winter, if New York offers nothing, migrate to Palm Beach or stand on the street corner while their wives go out to wash and scrub.[3] "An' it don't do fer me ter com-

3. Occupations in 1907 of 716 colored men (secured from records of the Young Men's Christian Association and personal visits) compared with census figures of occupations in 1900.

	716 Men	Census
Agricultural pursuits	—	1.2
Professional service, 27 men	3.8	3.6
Domestic and personal service, 363 men	50.6	58.1
5 barbers, 5 caterers, 24 cooks, 30 general utility men, 41 hotel men, 76 waiters and butlers, 8 valets, 35 janitors and sextons, 29 longshoremen, 5 laborers in tunnels, 7 asphalt workers, 57 elevator men, 41 laborers		
Trade and transportation, 279 men	39.0	28.4
10 chauffeurs, 35 drivers, 13 expressmen, 8 hostlers, 12 messengers, 14 municipal employees, 127 porters in stores, 15 porters on trains, 24 clerks, 21 merchants		
Manufacturing and mechanical pursuits, 47 men	6.6	8.7
	100.0	100.0

plain," one of them tells me, "else he gits 'high' an' goes off fer good." Waiters in restaurants sometimes do not make more than six dollars a week, to be supplemented by tips, bringing the sum up to nine or ten dollars. Hall men make about the same, but both waiters and hall men in clubs and hotels receive large sums in tips or in Christmas money. The Pullman car waiters have small wages but large fees.

Looking again at the census, we see that 129 out of every thousand janitors and sextons are colored. The janitor's position varies from the impecunious place in a tenement, where the only wage is the rent, to the charge of a large office or apartment building. Then come the laborers, nearly four thousand strong, with the elevator boy as a familiar figure. Forty per cent of the 139 laborers in my own tabulation were elevator boys, for, except in office buildings and large stores and hotels, this occupation is given over to the Negro, who spends twelve hours a day drowsing in a corner or standing to turn a wheel. Paul Lawrence Dunbar wrote poetry while he ran an elevator, and ambitious if less talented colored boys today study civil service examinations in their unoccupied time; but the situation as a life job is not alluring. Twenty-five dollars a month for wage, with perhaps a half this sum in tips, twelve hours on duty, one week in the nighttime and the next in the day—no wonder the personnel of this staff changes frequently in an apartment house. A bright boy will be taken by some businessman for a better job, and a lazy one drifts away to look for an easier task, or is dismissed by an irate janitor.

Quite another group of laborers are the longshoremen who, far from lounging indolently in a hallway, are straining every muscle as they heave some great crate into a ship's hold. The work of the New York dockers has been admirably described by Mr. Ernest Poole, who says of the thirty thousand longshoremen on the wharves of New York—Italians, Germans, Negroes, and Swedes, "Far from being the drunkards and bums that some people think them, they are like the men of the lumber camps come to town—huge of limb and tough of muscle, hard-swearing, quick-fisted, big of heart." Their tasks are heavy and irregular.

When the ship comes in, the average stretch of work for a gang
is from twelve to twenty hours, and sometimes men go to a
second gang and labor thirty-five hours without sleep. Their pay
for this dangerous, exhausting toil averages eleven dollars a week.
"There are thousands of Negroes on the docks of New York,"
Mr. Poole writes me, "and they must be able to work long hours
at a stretch or they would not have their jobs." At dusk, Brook-
lynites see these black, huge-muscled men, many of them West
Indians, walking up the hill at Montague Street. In New York
they live among the Irish in "Hell's Kitchen" and on San Juan
Hill. They are usually steady supporters of families.

New York demands strong, unskilled laborers. To some she
pays a large wage, and Negroes have gone in numbers into the
excavations under the rivers, though a lingering death may prove
the end of their two and a half or perhaps six or seven dollar
a day job. Many colored men worked in the subway during its
construction. One sees them often employed at rock drilling or
clearing land for new buildings. About a third of the asphalt
workers, making their two dollars and a half a day, are colored.
Some educated, refined Negroes choose the laborer's work rather
than pleasanter but poorly paid occupations. A highly trained
colored man, a shipping clerk, making seven dollars a week,
left his employer to take a job of concreting in the subway at
$1.80 a day. His decision was in favor of dirty, severe labor,
but a living wage.

When the next census is published, those of us who are carefully watching the economic condition of the Negro expect to
find a movement from domestic service into the positions of
laborers, including the porters in stores, who belong in our second
census division.

Kelly Miller[4] describes the massive buildings and sky-seeking
structures of our northern city, and finds no status for the Negro
above the cellar floor. One can see the colored youth gazing
wistfully through the office window at the clerk, whose business

4. Kelly Miller, *Race Adjustment,* p. 129.

reaches across the ocean to bewilderingly wonderful continents, knowing as he does that the employment he may find in that office will be emptying the white man's wastepaper basket.

TRADE AND TRANSPORTATION

	Total number of males in each occupation	Number of Negroes in each occupation	Number of Negroes to each 1000 workers in occupation
Agents—commercial travelers	27,456	67	2
Bankers, brokers, and officials of banks and companies	11,472	7	0
Bookkeepers—accountants	22,613	33	1
Clerks, copyists (including shipping clerks, letter and mail carriers)	80,564	423	5
Merchants (wholesale and retail)	72,684	162	2
Salesmen	45,740	94	2
Typewriters	3,225	36	11
Boatmen and sailors	8,188	145	18
Foremen and overseers	3,111	18	6
Draymen, hackmen, teamsters	51,063	1439	28
Hostlers	5,891	633	107
Livery stable keepers	967	9	9
Steam railway employees	11,831	70	6
Street railway employees	7,375	11	1
Telegraph and telephone operators	2,430	6	2
Hucksters and peddlers	12,635	69	5
Messengers, errand and office boys	13,451	335	25
Porters and helpers (in stores, etc.)	11,322	2143	188
Undertakers	1,572	15	9
Total, including some occupations not specified	405,675	5798	14

This, however, does not apply to government positions, and a large number of the 423 colored clerks in 1900 were probably in United States and municipal service. The latter we shall consider later as we study the Negro and the municipality. Of the former, in 1909 there were about 176 in the New York post offices.[5] Ambitious boys work industriously at civil service examinations, and a British West Indian will even become an American citizen for the chance of a congenial occupation. The clerkship, that to a white man is only a steppingstone, to a Negro is a highly coveted position.

I have made two divisions of this census list; the first includes those occupations requiring intellectual skill and carrying with them some social position, the second, those demanding only manual work. It is in the second that the colored man finds a place, and as a porter he numbers 2143, and reaches almost as high a percentage as the waiter and servant. Porters' positions are paid from five to fifteen dollars a week, the man receiving the latter wage performing also the duties of shipping clerk. There is some opportunity for advance, always within the basement, and there are regular hours and a fairly steady job.

The heading of draymen, hackmen, and teamsters, with twenty-eight colored in every thousand, shows that the Negro has not lost his place as a driver. The chauffeur does not appear in the census, but the Negro is steadily increasing in numbers in this occupation, and conducts three garages of his own.

The last census division to be considered in this chapter is that of manufacturing and mechanical pursuits.

When Mr. Stone wrote of the Southern states as the only place in which the Negro could "earn his bread in the sweat of his face," side by side with the white man, he must especially have been thinking of workers in the skilled trades. Unskilled laborers in New York are drenched in a common grimy fellowship. But in this last division the Negro is conspicuous by his absence.

5. It is difficult to get accurate figures as no official record is kept of color.

MANUFACTURING AND MECHANICAL PURSUITS

	Total number of males in each occupation	Number of Negroes in each occupation	Number of Negroes to each 1000 workers in occupation
Engineers, firemen (not locomotive)	16,579	227	14
Masons (brick and stone)	12,913	94	7
Painters, glaziers, and varnishers	27,135	177	6
Plasterers	4,019	51	12
Blacksmiths	7,289	29	4
Butchers	12,643	31	2
Carpenters and joiners	29,904	94	3
Iron and steel workers	10,372	40	4
Paper hangers	962	18	19
Photographers	1,590	22	14
Plumbers, gas and steam fitters	16,614	31	2
Printers, lithographers, and pressmen	21,521	53	2
Tailors	56,094	69	1
Tobacco and cigar factory operators	11,689	189	16
Fishermen and oystermen	1,439	65	45
Miners and quarrymen	326	21	64
Machinists	17,241	47	3
Total, including some occupations not specified	419,594	1774	4

Bakers, boot and shoe makers, gold and silver workers, brass workers, tin plate and tinware makers, box makers, cabinet makers, marble and stone cutters, bookbinders, clock and watch makers, confectioners, engravers, glass workers, hat and cap makers, and others—not more than nineteen in any one occupation, nor a higher per cent than four in a thousand.

Only four in every thousand where there should be eighteen! In Atlanta, under this division, the race reaches almost its due proportion, 279 in a thousand instead of 351. The largest number in any trade in New York is 189 men among the Cuban tobacco workers. Seventy-five per cent of all the masons in Atlanta are colored men, while in New York the colored are less than one per cent. Looking down the list we see that the figures are small and the percentage insignificant. The highly skilled and best-paid trades are seemingly as far removed from the Negro as the positions of floorwalkers or cashiers of banks.

Omitting for the present the professional class, we have reviewed the Negro as a worker, and neither in wages nor choice of occupation has he risen far to success. In domestic service he has gone a little down the ladder, serving in less desirable positions than in former years. Why has this happened? What good reasons are there for these conditions?

The first and most obvious reason is race prejudice. No display of talent, however prodigious, will open certain occupations to the colored race. As a salesman he could teach courteous manners to some of our white salesmen in New York, but he is never given a chance. There are a few Negroes, digging in the tunnels or sweeping down the subway stairs, who are capable of filling the clerkships that are counted the perquisites of the whites; but clerkships are only accessible as they are associated with municipal or federal service. Of course there are exceptions, and though they do not affect the rule, they show the existence of a few employers who ignore the color line, and a few Negroes of inexhaustible perseverance.

Mr. Stone argues that the Negro in the South profits by the strict drawing of the color line, since the white man, always considered the superior, is not lowered in the eyes of the community by working with the black man. The Southern white may lay bricks on the same wall with the Southern black, secure in his superior social position. But this seems fanciful as an explanation of labor conditions. The black doctor, for instance, in those localities where the color line is most rigid, may not ask the white doctor to consult with him; or if he does, his prompt removal from the community is requested. Colored postal clerks are in disfavor in the South, though not colored postmen. North or South, *the Negro gets an opportunity to work where he is imperatively needed*. Constituting one-third of the working population, he can make a place for himself in the laboring world of Atlanta as he cannot in New York. Pick up the twenty thousand New York Negroes and drop them in Liberia, and in two or three weeks Ellis Island could empty out sufficient men to fill their places; but remove a third of the male workers from Atlanta, and the city for years would suffer from the calamity. If they are the only available source of labor, colored men can work by the side of white men; but where the white man strongly dominates the labor situation, he tries to push his black brother into the jobs for which he does not care to compete.

We have seen, however, that in some occupations in New York the Negroes appear in such proportion as should be sufficient to secure them excellent positions; the most conspicuous instance being that of the two hundred colored waiters out of every thousand. Why, then, do we not see Negroes serving in the best hotels the city affords?

It has been an ideal of American democracy, a part of its strenuous individualism, that each member of the community should have full liberty in the pursuit of wealth. The ambitious, capable boy who walks barefooted into the city, and at the end of twenty years has outdistanced his country schoolmates, becoming a multimillionaire while they are still farm drudges, is the example of American opportunity. But this ability to separate one's self from the rest of one's fellows and attain individual greatness is rarely possible to a segregated race. In domestic service individual colored men have shown ambition and high capability, but they have never been able to get away from their fellows like the country boy—to leave the farm drudges and take a place among the most proficient of their profession. They must always work in a race group. And this Negro group is like the small college that tries to win at football against a competitor with four times the number of students and a better coach. The two hundred colored waiters, competing against the eight hundred white ones, lose in the game and are given a second place, which the best must accept with the worst. When, then, we criticize a capable colored man for failing to keep a superior position we must remember that he is tied to his group and has little chance of advancement on his individual merit.

The census division of mechanical pursuits shows only a few colored men working at trades, and the paucity of the numbers is often attributed by the Negro to a third obstacle in the way of his progress, the trade-union.

To the colored man who has overcome race prejudice sufficiently to be taken into a shop with white workmen, the walking delegate who appears and asks for his union card seems little short of diabolical; and all the advantages that collective bargaining has secured, the higher wage and shorter working day, are forgotten by him. I have heard the most distinguished of Negro educators, listening to such an incident as this, declare that he should like to see every labor union in America destroyed. But unionism has come to stay, and the colored man who is asked for his card had better at once get to work and endeavor to secure it. Many have done this already, and organized labor in New York, its leaders tell us, receives an increasing number of colored workmen. Miss Helen Tucker, in a careful study of Negro craftsmen in the West Sixties,[6] found among 121 men who had worked at their trades in the city, thirty-two, or 26 per cent, in organized labor. The majority of these had joined in New York. Eight men, out of the 121, had applied for entrance to unions and not been admitted. This does not seem a discouraging number, though we do not know whether the other eighty-one could have been organized or not. Many, probably, were not sufficiently competent workmen. In 1910, according to the best information that I could secure, there were 1358 colored men in the New York unions. Eighty of these were in the building

6. *Southern Workman,* October, 1907, to March, 1908.

trades, 165 were cigar workers, 400 were teamsters, 350 asphalt workers, and 240 rock drillers and tool sharpeners.[7]

Entrance to some of the local organizations is more easily secured than to others, for the trade-union, while part of a federation, is autonomous, or nearly so. In some of the highly skilled trades, to which few colored men have the necessary ability to demand access, the Negro is likely to be refused, while the less intelligent and well-paid forms of labor press a union

7. In 1906, and again in 1910, I secured a counting of the New York colored men in organized labor. The lists run as follows:

	1906	1910
Asphalt workers	320	350
Teamsters	300	400
Rock drillers and tool sharpeners	250	240
Cigar makers	121	165
Bricklayers	90	21
Waiters	90	not obtainable
Carpenters	60	40
Plasterers	45	19
Double drum hoisters	30	37
Safety and portable engineers	26	35
Eccentric firemen	15	0
Letter carriers	10	30
Pressmen	10	not obtainable
Printers	6	8
Butchers	3	3
Lathers	3	7
Painters	3	not obtainable
Coopers	1	2
Sheet metal workers	1	1
Rockmen	1	not obtainable
Total	1385	1358

The large number of bricklayers in 1906 is questioned by the man, himself a bricklayer, who made the second counting. However, the number greatly decreased in 1908 when the stagnation in business compelled many men to seek work in other cities.

card upon him. Again, strong organizations in the South, as the bricklayers, send men North with union membership, who easily transfer to New York locals. Miss Tucker finds the carpenters', masons', and plasterers' organizations easy for the Negro to enter. There is in New York a colored local, the only colored local in the city, among a few of the carpenters, with regular representation in the Central Federated Union. The American Federation of Labor in 1881 declared that "the working people must unite irrespective of creed, color, sex, nationality, or politics." This cry is for self-protection, and where the Negroes have numbers and ability in a trade, their organization becomes important to the white. It may be fairly said of labor organization in New York that it finds and is at times unable to destroy race prejudice, but that it does not create it.[8]

A fourth obstacle, and a very important one, is the lack of opportunity for the colored boy. The only trade that he can easily learn is that of stationary engineer, an occupation at which the Negroes do very well. Colored boys in small numbers are attending evening trade schools, but their chance of securing

8. The comment of the Negro bricklayer who secured my figures is important. "A Negro," he says, "has to be extra fit in his trade to retain his membership, as the eyes of all the other workers are watching every opportunity to disqualify him, thereby compelling a superefficiency. Yet at all times he is the last to come and the first to go on the job, necessitating his seeking other work for a living, and keeping up his card being but a matter of sentiment. While all the skilled trades seem willing to accept the Negro with his traveling card, yet there are some which utterly refuse him; for instance, the house smiths and bridge men who will not recognize him at all. While membership in the union is necessary to work, yet the hardest part of the battle is to secure employment. In some instances intercession has been made by various organizations interested in his industrial progress for employment at the offices of various companies, and favorable answers are given, but hostile foremen with discretionary power carry out their instructions in such a manner as to render his employment of such short duration that he is very little benefited. Of course, there are some contractors who are very friendly to a few men, and whenever any work is done by them, they are certain of employment. Unfortunately, these are too few."

positions on graduation will be small. The Negro youth who is not talented enough to enter a profession, and who cannot get into the city or government service, has slight opportunity. Nothing is so discouraging in the outlook in New York as the crowding out of colored boys from congenial remunerative work.

The last obstacle in the way of the Negro's advancement into higher occupations is his inefficiency. Race prejudice denies him the opportunity to prove his ability in many occupations, and the same spirit forces him to work in a race group; but the colored men themselves are often unfitted for any labor other than that they undertake.

The picture that is sometimes drawn of many thousands of highly skilled Southern colored men forced in New York to give up their trades and to turn to menial labor is not a correct one. Richard R. Wright, Jr., who has made a careful study of the Negro in Philadelphia,[9] finds that the majority of colored men who come to that city are from the class of unskilled city laborers and country hands; the minority are the more skillful artisans and farmers and domestic servants, with a number also of the vagrant and criminal classes.

In New York the untrained Negroes not only form a very large class, but coming in contact, as they do, with foreigners who for generations have been forced to severe, unremitting toil, they suffer by comparison. The South in the days of slavery demanded chiefly routine work in the fields from its Negroes.[10] The work was under the direction either of the master, the overseer, or a foreman; and there has been no general advance in training for the colored men of the South since that time. Contrast the intensive cultivation of Italy or Switzerland with the farms of Georgia or Alabama, or the hotels of France with those of Virginia, and you will see the disadvantages from which the Negro suffers. America is young and crude, but opportunity has

9. R. R. Wright, Jr., *Migration of Negroes to the North,* Annals of the American Academy, May, 1906.

10. See Ulrich B. Phillips' "Origin and Growth of the Southern Black Belts," *American Historical Review,* July, 1906.

brought to her great cities workmen from all over the world. In
New York these men are driven at a pace that at the outset
distracts the colored man who prefers his leisurely way. Moreover, the foreign workmen have learned persistence; they are
punctual and appear regularly each morning at their tasks. "The
Italians are better laborers than any other people we have, are
they not?" I asked a man familiar with many races and nationalities. "No," was his answer, "they do not work better than others,
but when the whistle blows, they are always there." Mr. Stone,
whose book I have already quoted a number of times, shows
the irresponsible, fanciful wanderings of his Mississippi tenants,
whom he endeavored, unsuccessfully, to establish in a permanent
tenantry. The colored men in New York are far in advance of
these farm hands, who are described as moving about simply
because they desire a change, but they are also far from the
steady, unswerving attitude of their foreign competitors. Inade-
quately educated, too often they come to New York with little
equipment for tasks they must undertake successfully or starve
—unless, puerile, they live by the labor of some industrious
woman.

I have tried to depict the New York colored wage earners
as they labor in the city today. They are not a remarkable
group, and were they white men, distinguished by some mark
of nationality, they would pass without comment. But the Negro
is on trial, and witnesses are continually called to tell of his
failures and successes. We have seen that both in the attitude of
the world about him, and in his own untutored self, there are
many obstacles to prevent his advance; and his natural sensitive-
ness adds to these difficulties. He minds the coarse but often
good-natured joke of his fellow laborer, and he remembers with
a lasting pain the mortification of an employer's curt refusal of
work. Had he the obtuseness of some Americans he would
prosper better. As we have seen, many positions are completely
closed to him, leading him to idleness and consequent crime.
Just as not every able-bodied white man, who is out of work
and impoverished, will go to the charities woodyard and saw

wood, so not every colored man will accept the menial labor which may be the only work open to him. Instead, he may gamble or drift into a vagabond life. A well-known Philadelphia judge has said that "The moral and intellectual advance of a race is governed by the degree of its industrial freedom. When that freedom is restricted there is unbounded tendency to drive the race discriminated against into the ranks of the criminal." Discrimination in New York has led many Negroes into these ranks. But as we look back at the occupations of our colored men we see a large number who secure regular hours, and if a poor, yet a fairly steady pay. For the mass of the Negroes coming into the city these positions are an advance over their former work. Employment in a great mercantile establishment, though it be in the basement, carries dignity with it, and educating demands of punctuality, sobriety, and swiftness. Richard R. Wright, Jr., whose right to speak with authority we have already noted, believes that the "North has taught the Negro the value of money; of economy; it has taught more sustained effort in work, punctuality, and regularity." It has also, I believe, in its more regular hours of work, aided in the upbuilding of the home.

I remember once waiting in the harbor of Genoa while our ship was taking on a cargo. The captain walked the deck impatiently, and, as the Italians went in leisurely fashion about their task, declared, "If I had those men in New York I could get twice the amount of work out of them." That is what New York does; it works men hard and fast; sometimes it mars them; but it pays a better wage than Genoa, and there is an excitement and dash about it that attracts laborers from all parts of the earth. The black men come, insignificant in numbers, ready to do their part. They work and play and marry and bring up children, and as we watch them moving to and from their tasks the North seems to have brought to the majority of them something of liberty and happiness.

CHAPTER FIVE

Earning a Living—
Business and
the Professions

IF WE WALK WEST on Fifty-ninth Street, at Eighth Avenue we come upon one of the colored business sections of New York. Here, for a block's length, are employment and real-estate agents, restaurant keepers, grocers, tailors, barbers, printers, expressmen, and undertakers, all small establishments occupying the first floor or basement of some tenement or lodging house, and with the exception of the employment agency all patronized chiefly by the colored race. Another such section and a more prosperous one is in Harlem, on West One Hundred and Thirty-third, One Hundred and Thirty-fourth, and One Hundred and Thirty-fifth streets. From the point of view of the whole business of the city such concerns are insignificant, but they are important from the viewpoint of Negro progress, since they represent the accumulation of capital, experience in business methods, and hard work. Very slowly the New York Negro is meeting the demanding power of his people and is securing neighborhood trade that has formerly gone to the Italian and the Jew. Husband and wife, father and son, work in their little establishments and make a beginning in the mercantile world.

The Negro, as we have seen, has conducted businesses in New

York in the past, businesses patronized chiefly by whites. Barbering and catering were his successes, and in both of these he has lost, despite the fact that one of the city's wealthiest colored men is a caterer. But if he has lost here, he has gained along other lines. Among a number of photographers he has one who is well known for his excellent architectural work. Two manufacturers have brought out popular goods, the Haynes's razor strop, and the Howard shoe polish. These men, one a barber and one a Pullman car porter, improved upon implements used in their daily work and then turned to manufacture. The headquarters of the Howard shoe polish is in Chicago, where the firm employs thirty people, the New York branch giving employment to twelve.

A wise utilization of labor already trained and at hand is seen in the Manhattan House Cleaning and Renovating Bureau. This firm contracts for the cleaning of houses and places of business and has also been successful in securing work on new buildings, entering as the builders leave and arranging everything for occupancy. In one week the Bureau has given employment to sixty men.

In those businesses in which he comes in contact with the white, the most pronounced success of the colored man has been real-estate brokerage. The New York Negro business directory names twenty-two real-estate brokers, and though a dozen of them probably handle altogether no more business than one white firm, a few put through important operations. The ablest of these brokers, recently clearing twenty thousand dollars at a single transaction, turned his operations to Liberia, where he went for a few months to look into land concessions. This broker has aided the Negroes materially in their efforts to rent apartments on better streets. His energy, and that of many more like him, is also needed to open up places for colored businesses, better office and workroom facilities for the able professional and business men and women. In New York as in the South the Negro needs to obtain a hold upon the land. In this he is aided not only by his brokers, but by realty companies. The largest of these, the Metropolitan Realty Company, in operation since 1900, is capitalized at a million dollars, and had in 1910

$400,000 paid in stock, and $400,000 subscribed and being paid for on installment. This company operates in the suburban towns, and has quite a colony in Plainfield, New Jersey, where it owns 150 lots. It has built eighty cottages for its members, and has bought eighteen.

Among the businesses that cater directly to the colored, probably none is more successful than undertaking. The Negroes of the city die in great numbers, and the funeral is all too common a function. Formerly this business went to white men, but increasingly it is coming into the hands of the colored. The Negro business directory gives twenty-two undertakers, one of them, by common report, the richest colored man in New York. Profitable real-estate investment, combined with one of the largest undertaking establishments in the city, has given him a comfortable fortune. Another large and increasingly important Negro business is the hotel and boardinghouse. As the colored men of the South and West accumulate wealth, they will come in increasing numbers to visit in New York, and the colored hotel, now little more than a boardinghouse, may become a spacious building, with private baths, elevator service, and a well-equipped restaurant. In today's modestly equipped buildings the catering is often excellent, and good, well-cooked food is sold at reasonable prices. Occasionally the Hotel Maceo advertises a Southern dinner, and its guests sit down to Virginia sugar-cured ham, sweet potato pie, and perhaps even opossum.

Printing establishments, tailors' shops,[1] express and van companies and many other small enterprises help to make up the Negro business world. One colored printer brings out an important white magazine. There are seven weekly colored newspapers, of which the New York *Age* is the most important, and two musical publishing companies. All these enterprises are useful, not only to the proprietor and his patrons, but especially to the clerks and assistants who thus are able to secure some training in mercantile work. In the white man's office, white and

---

1. On West One Hundred Thirty-third Street two former Hampton students have a prosperous little tailor and upholstering shop.

colored boys start out together, but as their trousers lengthen and their ambitions quicken, the former secures promotion while the latter is still given the letters to put into the mailbox. If the Negro lad, discouraged at lack of advancement, leaves the white man and ventures with a tiny capital into some business of his own, his ignorance is almost certain to lead to his disaster. He is indeed fortunate if he can first work in the office of a successful colored man.[2]

We have one more census division to consider, professional service. The table runs as follows:

PROFESSIONAL SERVICE

	Total number of males in each occupation	Number of Negroes in each occupation	Number of Negroes to each 1000 workers in occupation
Actors, professional showmen, etc.	4,733	254	54
Architects, designers, draftsmen	3,966	2	0
Artists, teachers of art	2,924	13	4
Clergymen	2,833	90	32
Dentists	1,509	25	16
Physicians and surgeons	6,577	32	5
Veterinary surgeons	320	2	6
Electricians	8,131	18	2
Engineers (civil) and surveyors	3,321	7	2
Journalists	2,833	7	2
Lawyers	7,811	26	3
Literary and scientific	1,709	10	5
Musicians	6,429	195	30
Officials (government)	3,934	9	2
Teachers and professors in colleges	3,409	32	9
Total including some occupations not specified	60,853	729	12

2. Those interested in the Negro in business should look for an intensive study, shortly to be published, on the wage earners and business enterprises among Negroes in New York. It is entitled *The Negro at*

Examining these figures we find few colored architects[3] or engineers, and a very small proportion of electricians, though among the latter there is a highly skilled workman. The New York Negro has no position in the mechanical arts. It may be that, as we so often hear, the African does not possess mechanical ability.[4] You do not see Negro boys puttering over machinery or making toy inventions of their own. But another and powerful reason for the colored youth's failing to take up engineering or kindred studies is the slight chance he would later have in securing work. No group of men in America have opposed his progress more persistently than skilled mechanics, and, should he graduate from some school of technology, he would be refused in office or workshop. So he turns to those professions in which he sees a likelihood of advancement.

Colored physicians and dentists are increasing in number in New York and throughout the country. The Negro is sympathetic, quick to understand another's feelings, and when added to this he has received a thorough medical training he makes an excellent physician. New York State examinations prevent the practice of ignorant doctors from other states, and the city can count many able colored practitioners. These doctors practice among white people as well as among colored. As surgeons they are handicapped in New York by lack of hospital facilities, having

---

Work in New York City, and has been made by George E. Haynes, under the direction of the Bureau of Social Research of the New York School of Philanthropy.

3. Since going to press the new and very beautiful building of St. Philip's Episcopal Church, on West One Hundred Thirty-fourth Street, has been opened. This is a fine example of English Gothic and its architects are two young colored men, one of whom was for years in the office of a white firm.

4. Mary Kingsley has some interesting generalizations on this point. She speaks of the African mind approaching all things from a spiritual point of view while the English mind approaches them from a material point of view, and of "the high perception of justice you will find in the African, combined with the inability to think out a pulley or a lever except under white tuition."—*West African Studies,* p. 330.

no suitable place in which they may perform an operation. The colored student who graduates from a New York medical college must go for hospital training to Philadelphia or Chicago or Washington.[5]

Colored lawyers are obtaining a firm foothold in New York. From twenty-six in the 1900 census they now, in 1911, number over fifty, though not all of these by any means rely entirely upon their profession for support. Some of our lawyers are descendants of old New York families, others have come here recently from the South.

Turning to our census figures again we see that the three professions in which the colored man is conspicuous are those of actor, musician, and minister. Instead of the average eighteen, he here shows fifty-four in every thousand actors, thirty in every thousand musicians, and thirty-two in every thousand clergymen. And since the pulpit and the stage are two places in which the black man has found conspicuous success it may be well in this connection to consider, not only the economic significance of these institutions, but their place in the life of the colored world.

The Negro minister was born with the Negro Christian, and the colored church, in which he might tell of salvation, is over a century old in New York. Today the Boroughs of Manhattan and Brooklyn have twenty-eight colored churches besides a number of missions. Some of the societies own valuable property, usually, however, encumbered with heavy mortgages, and yearly budgets mount up to ten, twelve, and sixteen thousand dollars. The Methodist churches lead in number, next come the Baptist, and next the Episcopalian. There are Methodist Episcopal, African Methodist Episcopal, and African Methodist Episcopal Zion.

5. Lincoln Hospital in New York, while receiving white and colored patients, was especially designed to help the colored race. It has a training school for colored nurses, but neither accepts colored medical graduates as interns, nor allows colored doctors upon its staff. This is one of many cases in which the good white people of the city are glad to assist the poor and ailing Negro, but are unwilling to help the strong and ambitious colored man to full opportunity.

Bethel African Methodist Episcopal Church, as we have seen, is one of the oldest and is still one of the largest and most useful Negro churches in New York. Mount Olivet, a Baptist church on West Fifty-third Street, has a seating capacity of 1600, taxed to its full on Sunday evenings. St. Philip's gives the Episcopal service with dignity and devoutness, and its choir has many sweet colored boy singers. At St. Benedict, the Moor, the black faces of the boy acolytes contrast with the benignant white-haired Irish priest, and without need of words preach good will to men. Only in this Catholic church does one find white and black in almost equal numbers worshiping side by side.

The great majority of the colored churches are supported by their congregations, and the minister or elder, or both, twice a Sunday, must call for the pennies and nickels, dimes and quarters, that are dropped into the plate at the pulpit's base. Contributors file past the table on which they place their offering, emulation becoming a spur to generosity. These collections are supplemented by sums raised at entertainments and fairs, and it is in this way, by the constant securing of small gifts, that the thousands are raised.

The church is a busy place and retains its members, not only by its preaching, but by midweek meetings. There are the class meetings of the Methodists, the young people's societies, the prayer meetings, and the sermons preached to the secret benefit organizations. Visiting sisters and brothers attend to relief work, and standing at a side table, sometimes picturesque with lighted lantern, ask for dole for the poor.

The Sunday schools, while not so large as the church attendance would lead one to expect, involve much time and labor in their conduct. A colored church member finds all his or her leisure occupied in church work. I know a young woman engaged in an exacting, skilled profession who spends her day of rest attending morning service, teaching in Sunday school, taking part in the young people's lyceum in the late afternoon, and listening to a second sermon in the evening. Occasionally she omits her dinner to hear an address at the colored Young

Men's Christian Association. On hot summer afternoons you may see colored boys and girls and men and women crowded in an ill-ventilated hall, giving ear to a fervid exhortation that leads the speaker, at the sentence's end, to mop his swarthy face. The woods, the salt-smelling sea, the tamer prettiness of the lawns of the city's park, have not the impelling call of sermon or hymn. If the whole of the Negro's summer Sunday is to be given to direct religious teaching, one wishes that it might take place at the old-time camp meeting, where there is fresh air and space in which to breathe it. The first of Edward Everett Hale's three rules of life as he gave them to the Hampton students was, "Live all you can out in the open air." The religious-minded New York Negro succumbs easily to disease, and yet elects to spend his day of leisure within doors.

With the exception of the Episcopalians, the churches undertake little institutional work. Money is lacking, and there is only a feeble conviction of the value of the gymnasium, pool table, and girls' and boys' clubs. The colored branches of the Young Men's Christian Association, however, are places for recreation and instruction. The lines that Evangelical Americans draw regarding amusements, prohibiting cards and welcoming dominoes, allowing bagatelle and frowning upon billiards, must be interpreted by some folklore historian to show their reasonableness. Doubtless the extent to which a game is used for gambling purposes has much to do with its good or bad savor, and pool and cards for this reason are tabooed. Dancing is also frowned upon by many of the churches, while temperance societies make active campaign for prohibition. To New York's black folk, the churchgoers and they who stand without are the sheep and the goats, and the gulf between them is digged deep.

Of the five colored Episcopal churches, St. Philip's and St. Cyprian's have parish houses. St. Philip's has moved into a new parish house on West One Hundred and Thirty-fourth Street, where with its large, well-arranged rooms, its gymnasium, and its corps of enthusiastic workers it will soon become a powerful force in the Harlem Negro's life. St. Cyprian's is under the City

Episcopal Mission, and has unusual opportunity for helpfulness since it is separated only by Amsterdam Avenue from the San Juan Hill district and yet stands amid the whites. Its clubs and classes, its employment agency, its gymnasium, its luncheons for school children, its beautiful church, are all primarily for the Negroes; but the colored rector has a friendly word for his white neighbors, towheaded Irish and German boys and girls sit upon his steps, and his ministry has lessened the belligerent feeling between the east and the west sides of Amsterdam Avenue. St. David's Episcopal Church in the Bronx has a fresh-air home at White Plains, cared for personally by the rector and his wife, who spend their vacation with tenement mothers and their children, the tired but grateful recipients of their good will.

If there were ninety colored clergymen in New York in 1900, as the census says, a number must have been without churches, itinerant preachers or directors of small missions, supporting themselves by other labor during the day. Those men who now fill the pulpits of well-established churches have been trained in theological schools of good standing, for the ignorant "darky" of the story who leaves the hot work of the cotton field because he feels a "call" to preach does not receive another from New York. The colored minister in this city works hard and long, and finds a wearying number of demands upon his time. The wedding and the funeral, the word of counsel to the young, and of comfort to the aged, a multiplicity of meetings, two sermons every Sunday, the continual strain of raising money, these are some of his duties. With a day from fourteen to seventeen hours long he earns as few men earn the meager salary put into his hand. But his position among his people is a commanding one, and carries with it respect and responsibility.

Strangers who visit colored churches to be amused by the vociferations of the preacher and the responses of the congregation will be disappointed in New York. Others, however, who attend, desiring to understand the religious teaching of the thoughtful Negro, find much of interest. They hear sermons marked by great eloquence. In the Evangelical church the preacher is not afraid to give his imagination play, and in finely chosen, vivid language, pictures his thought to his people. Especially does he love to tell the story of a future life, of paradise with its rapturous beauty of color and sound, its golden streets, its gates of precious stones, effulgent, radiant. He dwells not upon the harshness, but rather upon the mercy of God.

A theological library connected with a Calvinistic church, when recently catalogued, disclosed two long shelves of books upon hell and two slim volumes upon heaven. No such unloving puritanism dominates the Negro's thought. Hell's horrors may be portrayed at a revival to bring the sinner to repentance, but only as an aid to a clearer vision of the glories of heaven.

The Negro churches lay greater stress than formerly upon practical religion; they try to turn a fine frenzy into a determination for righteousness. This was strikingly exemplified lately in one of New York's colored Baptist churches. During the solemn rite of immersion the congregation began to grow hysterical, or "happy," as they would have phrased it; there were cries of "Yes, Jesus," "We're comin', Lord," and swayings of the body backward and forward. The minister with loud and stirring appeal for a time encouraged these emotions. Then in a moment he brought quiet to his congregation and called them to the consecration of labor. Faith without works was vain. Baptism was not the end, but only the beginning of their salvation. "You-all bleege ter work," he said, "if yer gwine foller der Lord. Ain't Jesus work in der carpenter shop till he nigh on thirty year old? Den one day he stood up (he ain't none er yer two-by-fo' men) an' he tak off his blue apun (I reckon he wore er apun like we-alls) an' he goes on down ter der wilderness, an' John der Baptist baptize him."

From oratory one turns naturally to music. The feeling for rhythm, for melodious sound, that leads the Negro to use majestic words of which he has not always mastered the meaning, leads him also to musical expression. He has an instinct for harmony, and, when within hearing distance of any instrument, will whistle, not the melody, however assertive, but will add a part.[6] Those who have visited colored schools, and especially the colored schools of the far South where the pupils are unfamiliar with other music than their own, can never forget the exquisite, haunting singing. When a foreman wants to get energetic work from his black laborers he sets them to singing stirring tunes. The Negro has his labor songs as the sailor has his chanties, and it would be impossible to measure the joy coming to both through musical expression.

In New York, despite their poverty, few Negroes fail to possess some musical instrument—a banjo perhaps, or a guitar, a mandolin or zither, or it may be the highly prized piano. Visiting of an evening in the Phipps model tenement, one hears a variety of gay tinkling sounds. And besides the mechanical instruments there is always the great natural instrument, the human voice. Singing, though not as common in the city as in the country, is still often heard, especially in the summer, and remains musical, though New York's noise and cheap and vulgar entertainments have an unhappy fashion of roughening her children's voices.

Music furnishes a means of livelihood to many Negroes and supplements the income of many others. Boys contribute to the family support by singing cheap songs in saloons or even in houses of prostitution. A boy "nightingale" will earn the needed money for rent while learning, all too quickly, the ways of viciousness. Others, more carefully reared, sing at church or secret society concert, perhaps receiving a little pay. Men form male quartets that for five or ten dollars furnish a part of an evening's entertainment. There are many Negro musicians and elocutionists who largely support themselves by their share in the receipts from concerts and social gatherings.

We speak of men crossing the line when they intermarry with the whites, but there is another crossing of the line when some Negro by his genius makes the world forget his race. Such a man is the artist, Henry Tanner; and New York has such Negro mu-

6. See H. J. Wilson, "The Negro and Music," *Outlook,* December 1, 1906.

sicians. Mr. Harry Burleigh, the baritone at St. George's, has won high recognition, not only as an interpreter, but as a composer of music; and one of the richest synagogues of the city has a Negro for its assistant organist. There are five colored orchestras in New York, the one conducted by Mr. Walter A. Craig having toured successfully in New England and many other Northern states.

But the colored musician has usually found his opportunity for expression and for a living wage upon the stage. Probably many of the actors noted on the census list are musicians, and many of the musicians, actors; the writer of the topical song having himself sung it in vaudeville or musical comedy. Few New Yorkers appreciate how many of the tunes hummed in the street or ground out on the hand organ, have originated in Negro brains. "The Right Church but the Wrong Pew," "Teasing," "Nobody," "Under the Bamboo Tree," which Cole and Johnson, the composers, heard the last thing as they left the dock in New York, and the first thing when they arrived in Paris, these are a few of the popular favorites. Handsome incomes have been netted by the shrewder among these composers, and the demand for their songs is continuous.

With a bright song and a jolly dance comes success. Picking up the copy of the New York *Age,* that lies on my desk, I find jottings of twenty-four colored troupes in vaudeville in the larger cities of the North and West. Three are at Proctor's and three at Keith's. Their economic outlook is not so hilarious as their songs, for transportation is expensive and bookings are uncertain; yet pecuniarily these actors are far better off than their more sober brothers who stick to their elevators or their porters' jobs.

Twenty years ago the Negro performer probably had little anticipation of advancing beyond minstrel work, in which he sang loud, danced hard, and told a funny story. S. H. Dudley, the leading comedian in the "Smart Set" colored company, said in 1909: "When I started in business I had no idea of getting as high as I am now. A minstrel company came to the little town in

Texas where I was raised, and at once my ambition fired me to become a musician. So I bought a battered horn and began to toot, to the great annoyance of my neighbors. Then I secured an engagement with a minstrel company whose cornet player had fallen into the hands of the law; and now here I am with one of the best colored shows ever gotten together and a starring tour arranged for next season." The movement from the minstrel show to the musical comedy, from the cheapest form of buffoonery to attractive farce, and even to good comedy, has been accomplished by a number of colored comedians. Williams and Walker may be considered the pioneers in this movement, and the story of their success, as Walker has told it, is a fine example of what the Negro can do along the line of decided natural aptitude. And it is important to notice this, for today, in the education of the race, aesthetic instincts are often suppressed with puritan vigor, and labor is made ugly and unwelcome.

Bert Williams and George Walker, one a British West Indian, the other a Westerner, met in California where each was hanging around a box manager's office, looking for a job. Hardly more than boys, they secured employment at seven dollars a week. That was in 1889. In 1908 they made each $250 a week, and in later times they have doubled and quadrupled this. Their first stage manager expected them to perform as the blacked-up white minstrels were performing, but the two boys soon saw that the Negro himself was far more entertaining than the buffoon portrayed by the white man. They wanted to show the true Negro, and billing themselves as the "real coons" (their white rivals called themselves "coons") they played in San Francisco with some success. Later they came to New York, and at Koster and Bial's made their first hit.

"Long before our run terminated," Walker said in telling of those early days, "we discovered an important fact: that the hope of the colored performer must be in making a radical departure from the old time 'darky' style of singing and dancing. So we set ourselves the task of thinking along new lines.

"The first move was to hire a flat in Fifty-third Street, furnish it, and throw our doors open to all colored men who possessed theatrical and musical ability and ambition. The Williams and Walker flat soon became the headquarters of all the artistic young men of our race who were stage-struck. We entertained the late Paul Lawrence Dunbar, who wrote lyrics for us. By having these men about us we had the opportunity to study the musical and theatrical ability of the most talented members of our race."

In 1893 the World's Fair was held at Chicago, and on the "Midway" the visitor saw races from all over the world. Here was a Dahomey village, with strange little huts, representative of the African home life. The Dahomeyans themselves were late in arriving, and American Negroes, sometimes with an added coat of black, were employed to represent them. Among them were Williams and Walker, who played their parts until the real Dahomeyans arriving, they became in turn spectators and studied the true African. This contact with the dancing and singing of the primitive people of their own race had an important effect upon their art. Their lyrics recalled African songs, their dancing took on African movements, especially Walker's. Anyone who saw Walker in "Abyssinia," the most African and the most artistic of their plays, must have recognized the savage beauty of his dancing when he was masquerading as an African king.

After the Dahomey episode the success of the two men was continuous. "In 1902 and 1903," Walker said, "we had all New York and London doing the cakewalk." In February, 1908, they appeared in "Bandanna Land," at the Majestic Theatre, and remained there for six months. Only those colored men who have made a steady, uphill struggle for the chance to play good comedy, know how important such recognition was for the Negro. "Bandanna Land" was probably the most popular light opera in New York that winter next to "The Merry Widow." The singing, especially that of the male chorus, was often beautiful. Mrs. Walker's dancing and charming acting were delightful, the chorus girls were above the average in beauty and musical expression, and the two men who made the piece were spontaneously, irresistibly funny; added to this, unlike its successful rival, "Bandanna Land" was without a vulgar scene or word.

This was the last time the two men played together. Walker became seriously ill, and died in January, 1911. After their company disbanded, Williams went back to the one-piece act of vaudeville, but as a star in a white troupe. His position as a permanent actor in the "Follies of 1910" marks a new departure for the colored comedian, a departure won by great talent combined with character and tact.

Since 1908 the Majestic has seen another colored company, Cole and Johnson's, presenting a half-Negro, half-Indian, musical comedy, the "Red Moon." These two men, for years in vaudeville, have written songs for Lillian Russell, Marie Cahill, Anna Held, and other popular musical comedy and vaudeville singers. They have played for six months continuously at the Palace Theatre, London. Accustomed to writing for white actors, their own plays are not so distinctively African as Williams and Walker's. Both Johnson and Cole are of the mulatto type, and neither blackens his face. Cole is one of the most amusing men in comedy in New York. He is tall and very thin, with a genius for finding lank and grotesque costumes that are delightfully incongruous with his grave face. The words of the musical comedies are his, the music, Johnson's. He, too, has become seriously ill, and his company has disbanded. In three years the colored stage has suffered serious loss, but we see forming new and successful companies whose reputation will soon be assured.

Comedy has always furnished a medium for criticism of the foibles of the times, and there are many sly digs at the white man in the colored play. Ernest Hogan, now deceased, better than anyone else played the rural southern darky. In the "Oysterman" we saw him in contact with a white scamp who was intent upon getting his recently acquired money. He was urged to take stock in a land company, to buy where watermelons grew as thick as potatoes, and chickens were as common as sparrows. The audience hated the white man heartily and sided with the simple, kindly, black youth, sitting with his dog at his side, on his cabin steps. Behind boisterous laughter and raillery the writers of these comedies often gain the sympathy of their hearers for the black race.

In this attempt to show the occupational life of the Negro, we have found that race prejudice often proves a bar to complete success, to full manhood. Something of this is true with the actor as well as with the laborer and the businessman. In securing entrance in vaudeville, color is at first an advantage. The "darky" to the white man is grotesquely amusing, and by rolling his eyes, showing a glistening smile, and wearing shoes that make a monstrosity of his feet, the Negro may create a laugh where the man with a white skin would be hooted off the stage. And since the laugh is so easily won, many colored actors become indolent and content themselves, year after year, with playing the part of buffoon. But with the ambition to rise in his profession comes the difficult struggle to induce the audience to see a new Negro in the black man of today. The public gives the colored man no opportunity as a tragedian, demanding that his comedy shall border always on the farcical. And what is demanded of the actor is also demanded of the musician. Writers of the scores of some of our musical comedies are musicians of superior training and ability, but rarely are they permitted full expression. Mr. Will Marion Cook, the composer of much of the music of "Bandanna Land," for a few moments gives a piece of exquisite orchestration. When the colored minister rises and exhorts his quarreling friends to be at peace with one another, one hears a beautiful harmony. I am told that Mr. Cook declares that the next score he writes shall begin with ten minutes of serious music. If the audience doesn't like it, they can come in late, but for ten minutes he will do something worthy of his genius.

However lighthearted a people, and however worthy of praise the entertainment that brings a jolly, wholesome laugh, let us hope that in the near future the Negro will find a more complete expression for his musical and histrionic gifts. Some actor of commanding talent, whose claims cannot be ignored, may reveal the larger life of the race. The nineteenth century knew a great Negro actor, Ira Aldridge, a *protégé* and disciple of Edmund Kean. He played Othello to Kean's Iago, and in the forties toured Europe with his own company, receiving high honors in Berlin and St. Petersburg.[7] A dark-skinned African, of immense power, physically and emotionally, he made Desdemona cry out in real fear, and caused Bassanio instinctively to shrink as he demanded his pound of flesh. Today's actor must be more subtle in his attack, but it may be given to him to reveal the thoughts at the back of the black man's mind. The genius of Zangwill gave us the picture of the children of the Ghetto; perhaps from the theater's seat the American will first understand the despised black race.

7. William J. Simmons, *Men of Mark.*

CHAPTER SIX

The Colored
Woman as a
Breadwinner

THE LIFE of the Negro woman of New York, if she belong to the laboring class, differs in some important respects from the life of the white laboring woman. Generalizations on so comprehensive a subject must, of course, meet with many exceptions, but the observing visitor, familiar with white and colored neighborhoods, quickly notes marked contrasts between the two, contrasts largely the result of different occupational opportunities. These pertain both to the married woman and the unmarried working girl.

The generality of white women in New York, wives of laboring men, infrequently engage in gainful occupations. In the early years of married life the wife relies on her husband's wage for support, and within her tiny tenement-flat bears and rears her children and performs her household duties—the sewing, cooking, washing, and ironing, and the daily righting of the contracted rooms. She is a conscientious wife and mother, and rarely, either by night or by day, journeys far from her own home. When unemployment visits the family wage earner, she turns to laundry work and day's cleaning for money to meet the rent and to supply the household with scanty meals; but as soon as her husband resumes work she returns to her narrow round of domestic duties.

After a score of these monotonous years more prosperous times come to the housewife. Every morning two or three children go out to work, and their wages make heavier the family purse. Son and daughter, having entered factory or store, bring home their pay envelopes unbroken on Saturday nights, and the augmentation of the father's wage gives the mother an income to administer. After the young people's wants in clothing and entertainment have been in part supplied, it becomes possible to buy new furniture on the installment plan, to hire a piano, even to move into a better neighborhood. The earnings of a number of children, supplementing the wage of the head of the family, make life more tolerable for all.

These days, however, do not last long. Sons and daughters marry and assume new responsibilities; the husband, his best strength gone, finds unemployment increasing; and since saving, except for wasteful industrial insurance, has seemed impossible without sacrificing the decencies and pleasures of the children, the end of the woman's married life is likely to be hard and comfortless.

This rough description may fairly be taken to represent the life of the average New York white woman of the laboring class. It is not, however, the life of the average colored woman. With her, self-sustaining work usually begins at fifteen, and by no means ceases with her entrance upon marriage, which only entails new financial burdens. The wage of the husband, as we have seen, is usually insufficient to support a family, save in extreme penury, and the wife accepts the necessity of supplementing the husband's income. This she accomplishes by taking in washing or by entering a private family to do housework. Sometimes she is away from her tenement nearly every day in the week; again the bulk of her earnings comes from home industry. Her day holds more diversity than that of her white neighbor; she meets more people, becomes familiar with the ways of the well-to-do—their household decorations, their dress, their refinements of manner; but she has but few hours to give to her children. With her husband she is ready to be friend and helpmate; but should he turn out a bad bargain, she has no fear of leaving him, since her marital relations are not welded by economic dependence. An industrious, competent woman, she works and spends, and in her scant hours of leisure takes pride in keeping her children well-dressed and clean.

At the second period of her married life, when her boys and girls, few in number if she be a New Yorker, begin to engage in self-supporting work, her condition shows less improvement than that of the white woman of her class. Sometimes her children hand her their whole wage, far oftener they bring her only such part as they choose to spare. The strict accounting of the minor to the parent, usual among Northerners in the past, and today common among the immigrant class, is not a part of the Negro's training. Rather, as the race has attained freedom it has copied the indulgent attitude of the once familiar "master," and regrets that its offspring must enter upon any work. Children with this tradition about them use the money they earn largely for the gratification of their vanity, not for the lessening of their mother's tasks. But a more potent factor than lack of discipline keeps the mother from being the administrator of the family's joint earnings. White boys and girls in New York enter work that makes it possible and advantageous for them to dwell at home; Negroes must go out to service, accept long and irregular hours in hotel or apartment, travel for days on boat or train. The family home is infrequently available to them, and money given in to it brings small return. Under these circumstances it is not strange if the mother must continue her round of washing and scrubbing.

The last years of life of the Negro woman, probably a little more than the last years of the white, are likely to bring happiness. With a mother at work a grandmother becomes an important factor, and elderly colored women are often seen bringing up little children or helping in the laundry—that great colored home industry. Accustomed all their lives to hard labor, it is easy for them to find work that shall repay their support, and in their children's households they are treated with respect and consideration.

The contrast in the lives of the colored and white married women is not more strongly marked than the contrast in the lives of their unmarried daughters and sisters. Unable to enter any pursuit except housework, the unskilled colored girl goes out to service or helps at home with the laundry or sewing. Factory and store are closed to her, and rarely can she take a place among other working girls. Her hours are the long, irregular hours of domestic service. She brings no pay envelope home to her mother, the two then carefully discussing how much belongs rightfully for board, and how much may go for the new coat or dress, but takes the eighteen or twenty dollars given her at the end of the month, and quite by herself determines all her expenditures. Far oftener than any class of white girls in the city she lives away from the parental home.

These are some of the differences found by the observer who looks into the Negro and the white tenement. They need not, however, rest alone upon any observer's testimony. We have in the census abundant statistics for their verification. Scattered among the volumes on population, occupations, and women at work are many facts concerning Negro women workers of New York, all of them confirmatory of the description just given. We may note the most important.

In 1900, whereas 4.2 per cent of the white married women in New York were engaged in gainful occupations, 31.4 per cent of the Negro married women were earning their living, over seven times as many in proportion as the whites.[1]

Again, in the total population of New York's women workers, 80 per cent were single, 10 per cent married, and 10 per cent widowed and divorced; while among the Negroes, the single

1. These figures are obtained by a combination of tables, one in Population, Vol. II, Part II, p. 332, describing the whole of Greater New York, the other in Women at Work, pp. 266 to 275, describing Manhattan, the Bronx, and Brooklyn. The error through the omission of Richmond and Queens is probably negligible.

women were only 53 per cent, the married 25 per cent, and the widowed 22.[2]

Statistics of the age period at which women are at work show the Negro's long continuing wage-earning activity. Between sixteen and twenty is a busy time for the women of both races. Among the whites 59 per cent are in gainful occupations, among the Negroes 66 per cent. But as the girl arrives at the period when she is likely to marry, the per cent of workers among the whites drops rapidly, until for white women, forty-five and over, it is 13.5, about one in seven. With the colored, among the women forty-five years of age and over, 53 per cent, more than half, still engage in gainful toil.[3]

Family life can be studied in the census table. While 59 per cent of the unmarried white girls at work live at home, this is found to be true of but 25 per cent of the colored girls; that is, 75 per cent, three-quarters of all the colored unmarried working women, live with their employers or board.[4]

The census volume on occupations reveals at once the narrow range of the New York colored woman's working life. Personal and domestic service absorbs 90 per cent of her numbers against 40 per cent among the white. But before considering more fully the colored girl at work, we need to notice another statistical fact, the preponderance in the city of Negro women over Negro men.

Like the foreigner, the youth of the Negro race comes first to the city to seek a livelihood. The colored population shows 41 per cent of its number between the ages of twenty and thirty-five. But unlike the foreigner, the Negro women find larger opportunity and come in greater numbers than the men. Their range of work is narrow, but within it they can command double the wages they receive at home, and if they are possessed of average

2. Federal Census 1900: Women at Work, Table 28, pp. 266 to 274. Among 800 married and widowed colored women whom I myself visited, I found only 150, 19 per cent, who were not engaged in gainful occupations.

3. Federal Census 1900: Women at Work, Table 10, pp. 147–151.

4. Federal Census 1900: Women at Work, Table 28, pp. 266–275.

ability, they are seldom long out of work. With the immense growth of wealth in New York the demand for servants continually increases, and finding little response from the white native-born population, many mistresses receive readily the services of the English-speaking Southern and West Indian blacks. So the boats from Charleston and Norfolk and the British West Indies bring scores and hundreds of Negro women from country districts, from cities where they have spent a short time at service, girls with and girls without experience, all seeking better wages in a new land.

Mr. Kelly Miller was the first to call attention to the presence in American cities of surplus Negro women.[5] The phenomenon is not peculiar to New York. Baltimore, Washington, New Orleans, all show the same condition. In Atlanta the women number 143 to every hundred colored men. New York shows 123 to every masculine one hundred. These surplus women account in part for the number of Negro women workers in New York not living at home. Some are with their employers, but others lodge in the already crowded tenements, for the Southern servant, unaccustomed to spending the night at her employer's, in New York also, frequently arranges to leave her mistress when her work is done. In their hours of leisure the surplus women are known to play havoc with their neighbors' sons, even with their neighbors' husbands, for since lack of men makes marriage impossible for about a fifth of New York's colored girls, social disorder results. Surplus Negro women, able to secure work, support idle, able-bodied Negro men. The lounger at the street corner, the dandy in the parlor thrumming on his banjo, means a Malindy of the hour at the kitchen washboard. In a town in Germany, where men were sadly scarce, I was told that a servant girl paid as high as a mark to a soldier to walk with her in the Hofgarten on a Sunday afternoon. Colored men in New York command their "mark," and girls are found who keep them in polished boots,

5. This is incorporated in a chapter in Mr. Miller's volume on *Race Adjustment*.

fashionable coats, and well-creased trousers. Could the Negro country boy be as certain as his sister of lucrative employment in New York, or could he oftener persuade her to remain with him on the farm, he would better city civilization. But the demand for servants increases, and the colored girl continues to be attracted to the city where she can earn and spend.

The table that appears below shows in condensed form the occupations of the Negro women in New York. As we see, the Negro women number forty-four in every thousand women workers.

Ninety per cent of all the Negro women workers of New York are in domestic and personal service. This includes a

FEMALES TEN YEARS OF AGE AND OVER, ENGAGED IN GAINFUL OCCUPATIONS IN NEW YORK

	Total	Negro	Number to every 1000 workers
Professional service	22,422	281	12
Domestic and personal service	146,722	14,586	100
Laundresses	16,102	3,224	200
Servants and waitresses	103,963	10,297	99
All others	24,657	1,065	43
Trade and transportation	65,318	106	Between one and two
Manufacturing and mechanical pursuits	132,535	1,138	7
Dressmakers	37,514	813	22
Seamstresses	18,108	249	14
All others	76,913	76	1
Total including some occupations not specified	367,437	16,114	44

Federal Census 1900: Occupations, Table 43, p. 638.

variety of positions. Some Negro girls work in stores, dusting stock, taking charge of cloak or toilet rooms, scrubbing floors. Their hours are regular, but the pay, five or six, or very occasionally eight dollars a week, means a scanty livelihood without hope of advancement. The position of maid in a theater where perquisites are larger is prized, and a new and pleasant place is that of a maid on a limited train. But the bulk of the girls are servants in boardinghouses, or are with private families as nurses, waitresses, cooks, laundresses, maids-of-all-work, earning from sixteen and eighteen to twenty-five and even thirty dollars a month. Occasionally a very skillful cook can command as high a monthly wage as fifty dollars.

The colored girl is frequently found engaged at general housework in a small apartment. Her desire to return to her lodging at night makes her popular with families living in contracted space. With the conveniences of a New York flat, dumb-waiter, clothes dryer, gas, and electricity, general housework is not severe. Work begins early, seven at the latest, and lasts until the dinner is cleared away, at half-past eight or nine. Released then from further tasks, the young girl goes to her tiny inner tenement room, dons a fresh dress, and then, as chance or her training determines, walks the streets, goes to the theater, or attends the class meeting at her church. Entertainments among the Negroes are rarely under way until ten o'clock, and short hours of sleep in ill-ventilated rooms soon weaken the vitality of the newcomer. Housework under these conditions does not create much ambition; the mistress moves, flitting, in New York fashion, from one flat to another, and the girl also flits among employers, changing with the whim of the moment.

Few subjects present so fascinating a field for discussion as domestic service, and the housewife of today enters into it with energy, sometimes decrying the modern working girl, again planning household economics that shall lure her from factory or shop. The only point we need to consider now is the dissatisfaction that results when 64 per cent of the women of a race are forced by circumstances into one occupation. Those with native ability along this line succeed and make others and themselves happy. The faithful, patient, loyal Negro servant is well known, the black mammy has passed into American literature, but not every colored woman can wisely be given this position.

Some of the Negro girls who take up housework in New York are capable of more intelligent labor, and chafe under their limitations; others have not the ability to do good housework; for domestic service requires more mental capacity than is demanded in many factories. In short, a great many colored girls in New York are round pegs in square holes, and the community is the loser by it.

Among these round pegs are girls who, determining no longer to drudge in lonely kitchens, contrive, as we shall see later, to find positions at other more attractive reputable work. Others, deciding in favor of material betterment at whatever cost, lower their moral standard and secure easier and more remunerative jobs. A well-paying place, with short hours and high tips, at once offers itself to the colored girl who is willing to work for a woman of the demimonde. In the sporting house also she is preferred as a servant, her dark complexion separating her from other inmates. In 1858, Sanger wrote in his *History of Prostitution,* "The servants (in these houses) are almost always colored women. Their wages are liberal, their perquisites considerable, and their work light." Untrained herself, bereft of home influence, with an ancestry that sometimes cries out her parents' weakness in the contour and color of her face, the Negro girl in New York, more even than the foreign immigrant, is subject to degrading temptation. The good people, who are often so exacting, want her for her willingness to work long hours at a lower wage than the white; and the bad people, who are often so carelessly kind, offer her light labor and generous pay. It is small wonder that she sometimes chooses the latter.

Not all the colored girls who work in questionable places and with questionable people take the jobs from choice; some are sent without knowing the character of the house they enter. A few years ago an agitation was started for the protection of helpless Negro immigrants who had fallen into the hands of unscrupulous employment agencies. A system existed, and still exists, by which employment agencies were able to advance the traveling expenses of Southern girls, who on their arrival in New York were held in debt until the cost of the journey had been many times repaid. Helpless in the power of the agent, the newcomer was forced to work where he wished. Under the city's department of licenses some of the more unscrupulous of these agencies have been closed, and philanthropy has placed a visitor at the docks to give aid and advice to unprotected girls. But the danger is by no means over. Those familiar with the subject assert that there is a proportionately larger black slave than white slave traffic.

There is a gainful occupation for women, black and white, too important to be left unnoticed. The census does not tabulate it. The best people strive to ignore it, and carefully sheltered girls grow up unconscious of its existence. But the employment agent understands its commercial value, and little children in the red light neighborhood are as familiar with it as with the vending of peanuts on the street. To the poor it is always an open door affording at least a temporary respite from dispossession and starvation. How many of the colored turn to it, we do not know—certainly not a few. Some gain from it a meager livelihood, but others, for a time at least, achieve comfort and even luxury.

Among the round pegs that the square holes so uncomfortably chafe are colored girls of intelligence and charm who deliberately join the antisocial class. Probably a few in any case would lead this life, but the history of many shows an unsuccessful struggle for congenial work, ending with a choice of material comfort however high the moral cost. In One Hundred and Thirty-fourth and One Hundred and Thirty-fifth streets are apartments where such girls live, two or three together, surrounded by comforts that their respectable neighbors who go out to cook, wash, and iron may fruitlessly long for all their lives. A colored philanthropic worker, stopping by chance at the door of one of these places, saw an old college friend. "How can you do it!" she cried as she recognized the life the girl was leading, "How can you do it! I would rather kill myself scrubbing!" "There is the difference between us," came the answer, "I am not willing to die, and I cannot and will not scrub."

It is pleasant and encouraging to turn from colored women

who have given up the struggle, to ambitious, successful workers. Some among these are in the domestic service group and enjoy with heartiness their tasks as nursemaid or cook. "This is my piano day," an expert colored washerwoman says of a Monday morning. Among the domestic service workers, as classified by the census, is the trained nurse, filling an increasingly important position in New York. In 1909, Lincoln Hospital graduated twenty-one colored nurses, some of whom remain in New York to do excellent work.

In the professions, with the women as with the men, the first place numerically is occupied by performers upon the stage. So much has been said of the Negro as an actor that there is little to add. A rather better class of colored than of white women join musical comedy chorus troupes, for fifteen or eighteen dollars a week that will attract a Negro to the stage can be made by a white girl in a dozen other ways. Lightness of color seems a requisite for a stage position, unless a dark skin is offset by very great ability, as in the case of Aida Walker, one of the most graceful and charming women in musical comedy.

No record is kept of the number of colored teachers in the city's public schools, but each year Negro graduates from the normal college secure positions. These are found from the kindergarten through the primary and up to the highest grammar grade. The colored girl with intellectual ability, particularly if she comes of an old New York family, is apt to turn to teaching. Her novitiate is long, but a permanent certificate secured, she is sure of a good salary, increasing with her years of service, and ending in a pension. This path of security has perhaps tended to keep New York colored girls from going into other lines of work. I have not yet found one who has graduated from a university. Pratt Institute and the Teachers' College have colored normal students, but they are usually from the South or West, not New Yorkers born.

Philanthropy is opening up important lines of opportunity to the Negro woman in New York. In 1903, a colored graduate nurse secured an interview with the Secretary of the New York

Charity Organization Society, and so ably presented to him the need of Negro visitors among Negroes that she was appointed visiting nurse for the colored sick who came under the notice of the Society. In time the position changed into that of a colored district visitor, other colored nurses entering in numbers into district nursing work. In 1910, three nurses were employed by the Nurses' Settlement, two by the Association for Improving the Condition of the Poor of Manhattan, and two by the District Nursing Association of Brooklyn. With increased knowledge of the sickness and suffering amid the Negro poor, and of their need of proper care in their homes, the number of these nurses will doubtless increase. Colored women rank high among the trained nurses of New York.

Other philanthropic work lately has been undertaken by Negro women in New York. In 1910, besides the nurses of whom we have spoken, there were at the head of societies in salaried positions, two settlement workers, two matrons of day nurseries, two matrons of homes in which much social work was carried on, many employees in colored orphan asylums, a teacher of domestic science in a homekeeping flat, a traveler's aid visitor, a playground instructor, besides workers in various religious organizations. This does not include the many colored women doing social and recreation work in the public schools and on the city's playgrounds. Indeed, the difficulty in New York is to secure trained colored women for philanthropic work, the Negro's attitude still being that of the great majority of white women a few years ago, that love for children and a sentimental kindness constitute the requisites for work among the poor. But the school of experience is training workers, and as the schools of philanthropy of New York, Boston, and Chicago also graduate colored students, we shall have in the North the intelligent, trained workers whom we need.

The little kindergarten girl who, with head erect, walked past the jeering line of boys to the green trees and soft grass of the park has her counterpart in many young women of New York. In 1909, a colored girl graduated from one of the city's dental colleges, the first woman of her race to take this degree in the state. From the first her success was remarkable. Colored girls with ability and steady purpose and dogged determination have won success in clerical and business work; but the last large and efficient group is that classified in the census under mechanical and manufacturing pursuits: the dressmakers, seamstresses, milliners.

Colored women have always been known as good sewers, and recently they have studied at their trade in some of the best schools. From 1904 to 1910, the Manhattan Trade School graduated thirty-four colored girls in dressmaking, hand sewing, and novelty making. The public night school on West Forty-sixth Street, under its able colored principal, Dr. W. L. Bulkley, since 1907, has educated hundreds of women in sewing, dressmaking, millinery, and artificial flower making. While the majority of the pupils have taken the courses for their private use, a large minority are entering the business world. They meet with repeated difficulties; white girls refuse to work in shops with them, private employers object to their color, but they have, nevertheless, made creditable progress. The census reports the number of Negro dressmakers to have quadrupled in the United States from 1890 to 1900. Something comparable to this increase in dressmaking and allied trades has taken place among the Negroes of New York, and it has come through education and persistence, and the increase of trade among the colored group itself. Numbers of these dressmakers and milliners earn a livelihood, though often a scanty one, from the patronage of the people of their own race.

But despite her efforts and occasional successes, the colored girl in New York meets with severer race prejudice than the colored man, and is more persistently kept from attractive work. *She gets the job that the white girl does not want.* It may be that the white girls want the wrong thing, and that the jute mill and tobacco shop and flower factory are more dangerous to health and right living than the mistress' kitchen, but she knows her mind, and follows the business that brings her liberty of action when the six o'clock whistle blows. What she desires for herself, however, she refuses to her colored neighbor. Occasionally an employer objects to colored girls, but the Manhattan Trade School repeatedly, in trying to place its graduates, has found that opposition to the Negro has come largely from the working girls. Race prejudice has even gone so far as to prevent a colored woman from receiving home work when it entailed her waiting in the same sitting room with white women. Of course, this is not the universal attitude. In friendly talks with hundreds of New York's white women workers, I have found the majority ready to accept the colored worker. Jewish girls are especially tolerant. They believe that good character and decent manners should count, not color; but an aggressive, combative minority is quite sure that no matter how well educated or virtuous she may be, no black woman is as good as a white one. So the few but belligerent aristocrats triumph over the many half-ashamed, timid democrats.

The shirtwaist makers' strike of 1910 was so profoundly important in its breaking down of feeling between nationalities, its union of all working women in a common cause, that the colored girl, while very slightly concerned in the strike itself, may profit by the more generous feeling it engendered. Certainly an entrance into store and workshop would be to her immense advantage. She needs the discipline of regular hours, of steady training, of order and system. She needs also to become part of a strong labor group, to share its working class ideal, to feel the weight of its moral opinion; instead of looking into the mirror of her wealthy mistress, she needs to reflect the aspirations of the strong, earnest women who toil.

Before bringing the story of the life of the New York colored working woman to a close, it may not be amiss to look closely at the discrimination practiced against her, not only in her work, but in her daily life. The Negro comes North and finds himself half a man. Does the woman, too, come to be but half a woman? What is her status in the city to which she turns for opportunity and larger freedom?

Four years ago, within a few hours' time, two stories were told me, illustrative of the colored woman's status. Neither occurred in the city of New York, but both are indicative of its temper. The first I heard from a woman skilled in a difficult profession, a Canadian now residing in the United States, and the descendant of a fugitive slave. Her youthful companions had all been white, and while an African in the darkness of her skin and her musical voice, her rearing had been that of an Englishwoman. "Shortly after coming to New York, I went for the first time," she told me, "to a little resort on the Jersey coast. A board walk flanked the ocean, and on the other side were shops and places of amusement. Going out one morning with two companions, a colored man and woman, we turned into an enclosure to examine a gaily painted merry-go-round. The place was open to the public, and a few nursery maids with their charges were seated about. The man in our party, interested in the mechanism of the machine, went up to it and began to explain it to us. Quite suddenly a rough fellow, in charge of the place, walked over and called out, 'Get out of here! We don't allow niggers.' The attack, to me at least, was so overwhelming that I did not move at once. Thereupon I was again called 'nigger,' and ordered out.

"When I reached the beach, I asked my companions to leave me, and I sat on a bench looking upon the waves. After a time an old woman came to my side, and said a little timidly, 'What are you thinking about, dearie?' Looking in her face I saw that she feared that I would commit suicide. 'I am thinking,' I said turning to her, 'that I wish the ocean might rise up and drown every white person on the face of the earth.' 'Oh, you mustn't say that,' she cried horrified, and left me. After I cannot tell how many minutes or hours, I returned to my boardinghouse, and then to my home in New York. I had had a great many white friends in my native home; I had played with them, eaten with them, slept with them. Now I destroyed their letters, and resolved never to know them again. That was my first affront in the United States, and while I have learned to feel somewhat differently, a little to discriminate, I can never forget that the white people in the North stand for the insult which was cast upon me."

On the evening of the same day I had learned of this happening, a man from a prominent college in New York State told me of a Negro classmate. "He was a pleasant, intelligent fellow from the South," he said, "and while I never knew him well, I was always glad to see him. One day, at commencement time, when we were all having our relatives about, he boarded my car with a young colored woman, evidently his sister. Without a thought I rose, lifted my hat, and gave her my seat. Never again shall I see such a look of gratitude as that which lighted up his face when he bowed in acknowledgment of my courtesy. It revealed the race question to me, and yet I had performed only the simplest act of a gentleman."

In these two incidents we see the undecided, perplexing position of the Negro woman in New York. Today she may be turned out of a public resort as a "nigger," tomorrow she may receive the dues of a gentlewoman. And since, while I write, I hear the cry of a class in the community who adjudge the expulsion necessary since the other course must lead at once to social equality, I make haste to add that the second story did not end in wedlock. As far as I have seen, it never does. Intermarriage of white and black in New York is so slight as to be a negligible quantity, but amalgamation between the two races is not uncommon. And this we may say with certainty, the man most blatant against the "nigger" in New York as all over the country is the man most ready to enter into illicit relationship with the woman whom he claims to despise. The raising of the hat to the colored woman brings a diminution in sexual immorality.

If the Negro civilization of New York is to be lifted to a higher level, the white race must consistently play a finer and more generous part toward the colored woman. There are many inherent difficulties against which she must contend. Slavery deprived her of family life, set her to daily toil in the field, or appropriated her mother's instincts for the white child. She has today the difficult task of maintaining the integrity and purity of the home. Many times she has succeeded, often she has failed, sometimes she has not even tried. A vicious environment has strengthened her passions and degraded her from earliest girlhood. Beyond any people in the city she needs all the encouragement that philanthropy, that human courtesy and respect, that the fellowship of the workers can give—she needs her full status as a woman.

CHAPTER SEVEN

Rich and Poor

O F THE MANY NATIONS AND RACES that dwell in New York none, with the exception of the Chinese, is so aloof from us in its social life as the Negro. The childish recollection of an old school friend, recently related to me, well illustrates this. Across the way from where she lived there was a house occupied by a family of mulattoes. They were the quietest and least obtrusive people on the block, and the wife, who was known to be very beautiful, on the rare occasions when she left her home, was always veiled. The husband was little seen, and the child, a shy boy, never played on the street. For years the family lived aloof from their neighbors, the subject of hushed and mysterious questioning.

Probably had one of the white women dropped in some day to say good morning or to borrow a recipe book, the mystery would have been wholly dispelled—a pity surely for the children Few of New York's citizens are so American as the colored, few show so little that is unusual or picturesque. The educated Italian might have in his home some relic of his former country, the Jew might show some symbol of his religion; but the Negro, to the seeker of the unusual, would seem commonplace. The colored man in New York has no associations with his ancient African home, no African traditions, no folklore. The days of slavery he wishes completely to forget, even to the loss of his exquisite plantation music. He is ambitious to be conventional in his manners, his customs, striving as far as possible to be like his neighbor—a distinctly American ambition. In consequence, after indicating the lines along which he has achieved economic success, one finds little to describe in the lives of the well-to-do that will be of interest. And yet this sketch would be open to criticism if, after so long a survey of the working class, it gave no space to those Negroes who have achieved a fair degree of wealth and leisure; and perhaps the very recital of the likeness of these people to those about them may be of importance, for the great mass of white Americans are like a vivacious Kentuckian of my acquaintance, who, on learning something of a well-to-do Negro family, assured me that she knew less of such people than she did of the Esquimaux.

Mr. William Archer, in his book, *Through Afro-America,* describes a round of visits to Southern Negro homes, where, with touching pride, his hostesses show their material wealth, or rather the material wealth of their race as embodied in drawing room, dining room, and bedroom. There seemed to be nothing remarkable about the rooms unless their very existence was remarkable. So the interiors of colored homes in New York would reveal nothing to mark them from the homes of their neighbors, save perhaps the universal presence of some musical instrument. In Brooklyn, the Bronx, and in the Jersey suburbs, Negroes buy and rent houses, sometimes with a few of their race in close proximity, sometimes with white neighbors only on the block. Brooklyn seems always to have shown less race antagonism than Manhattan (where, indeed, anything but the apartment is beyond the pocketbook of people of modest means), and it has been in Brooklyn for the past three generations that the well-to-do colored families with their children have chiefly been found.

Much pleasant hospitality and entertainment take place behind these modest doors. Visitors are common, relatives from the east and west and south, and little dinner and supper parties are numerous. If church discipline does not interfere, the women have their afternoons of whist, and despite church discipline, dancing is very common, few entertainments proving successful without it. To play well upon some musical instrument is almost a universal accomplishment, and, as with the Germans, families and friends meet the oftener for this harmonious bond.

The social life of the well-to-do colored family generally centers about the church, and with a regularity unusual among the white people, father and mother and children attend the Sunday and weekday meetings. Colored society is also at the period of the bazaar and fair, the concert and dramatic entertainment. Money is raised by this means for the church, the private charity, or to supplement the dues of the mutual benefit society. There are a number of Negroes in the different large cities who support themselves by concerts and readings, appearing at benefits in the North and South, where they receive a third or a half of the receipts. Amateur performances are also common. A young New York college man, one winter evening, saw two refined, remarkably well-dressed colored women turn in at the entrance of the Grand Central Palace. Purchasing a ticket for the benefit, as it proved, of a colored day nursery (the entertainment netted $2300), he followed them to find himself in the Afro-American social world. For while the amateur dancing and singing upon the stage were pretty and attractive, the young man was far more interested in the audience. "And the disappointing thing about it," he remarked in telling of it afterwards, "was that they were exactly like other people." To use the newspaper phrase, "there was no 'story.' " They were a group of Americans, trained in the social conventions of their own land.

There are many secret and benefit societies among the Negroes in New York. The Masons have nine meeting places; the Elks, ten lodges. The Odd Fellows have twenty-two places of meeting. The United Order of True Reformers, a strong Negro organization in the South, where it conducts large business enterprises, has forty-four headquarters in church and hall and private house, where meetings are held twice a month. Many benefit societies are closely associated with the churches. Colored men and women are very busy with their multitudinous church and society and benefit meetings. I remember once attending an evening service at a colored church when the minister preached the sermon to the benefit orders of St. Luke's and the Galilean Fishermen. The officers, some of them carrying spears with blue and red and white trimmings, marched down the aisle and took their seats at the front of the pulpit. Their leader was in purple, wearing a huge badge like a breastplate with yellow and green stones. The women, equally prominent with the men, were dressed one in yellow with green over it, and broad purple bands, two in white with golden crowns. The pageant was very pretty, even beautiful, but too artless in its simple enjoyment of color and display for the conventional society of New York, and the colored "four hundred" were not in it.

Who are the four hundred in New York's colored society? An outsider would be very bold who should attempt to answer. Twenty-five years ago the New Yorker born, especially the descendant of some prominent antislavery worker, would have held foremost social position. The taint of slavery was far removed from these people, who looked with scorn upon arrivals from the South. Many were proud of their Indian blood, and told of the freedom that came to their black ancestors who married Long Island Indians. But these old New York colored families, sometimes bearing historic Dutch and English names, have diminished in size and importance as have the old white families beside them. The younger generation has gone west, or has died and left no issue. And into the city has come a continual stream of Southerners and more recently West Indians, some among them educated, ambitious men and women, full of the energy and determination of the immigrant who means to attain to prominence in his new home. These newcomers occupy many of the pulpits, are admitted to the bar, practice medicine, and become leaders in politics, and their wives are quite ready to take a prominent part in the social world. They meet the older residents, and the various groups intermingle, though not without some friction. Like a country village, the New York Negro social world knows the happenings of its neighbors, gossips over their shortcomings, rejoices, though with something of jealousy, over their successes, and has its cliques, its many leaders, but also its broad-minded spirits who strive to bring the whole village life into harmony.

As we have learned from a study of the occupational life of the Negro, the majority of men and women of means are in the professional class, or in the city or federal service. Such positions do not carry with them large incomes, and remembering the high cost of living in New York, and the exorbitant rental paid by black men, we can see that, gauged by the white man's standard, the Negro with his two or three or four thousand dollars a year is poor. Yet with his very limited income the demands upon him are enormous. In the first place, he must educate his children, and this means a large expenditure, for only in the technical schools or the college can his boy or girl be prepared for a successful career. The white boy may find some business firm that will give him a chance of advancement, but the colored boy must receive such an education as shall fit him to start an enterprise by himself, unless he enters public service. So the trade or professional school or college absorbs the savings of many years.

The church is another large recipient of the Negro's slender means. Watching the dimes and quarters drop into the contribution plate as the dark-faced congregation files past the pulpit on a Sunday evening, one wonders whether any other people in America willingly give so large an amount of their income to their religious organizations. And not only will money be requested for the church's need, but special offerings will be given to home and foreign mission work. In 1907, the African Methodist Church alone raised $36,000 for home and foreign missions. The Baptists raised $44,000. Educational work demands a share: the African Methodists support twenty schools, the African Zion twelve, and the Negro Baptists one hundred and twenty. The other denominations do their share, and the Negroes also give to the schools conducted by white churches for their people. This money comes from all over the country, and the well-to-do New York Negro must contribute his part.

Home charities also help to drain the Negro's purse. Manhattan and Brooklyn have a number of colored philanthropies, orphan asylums, old people's homes, rescue missions, Young Men's and Young Women's Christian Associations, and social settlements. Some are supported entirely by white people, but the greater number receive some contributions from the colored, and a few are dependent for money upon that race alone. Thousands of dollars are raised yearly, among the well-to-do New York Negroes, for these institutions.

Yet, with all these various philanthropic activities, one too frequently hears that the Negro does not support his own charities. As though anything of the sort could be expected of him! A little time ago, in asking for money for settlement work among Negroes, I was asked in turn by the exquisitely dressed woman before me, whose furs and gown and jewels must have represented a year's salary of a schoolteacher, the type of wealthy woman among the colored, why the well-to-do Negroes did not support the settlement themselves. No such question is asked when we demand money for work among the Italians or the Jews, who have incomparably larger means. Indeed, one may question whether the Negro is not too generous for the materialistic city of New York, whether his successes would not be greater were he niggardly toward himself and others. He lives well, dresses well, enjoys a good play, strives to give every advantage to his children, helps the poor of his race. To hold his own today in this civilization, he needs to be taught to seek first riches, waiting until much treasure has been laid up before he allows philanthropy to draw upon his bank account.

The traveler to the British West Indies finds three divisions among the inhabitants, white, colored, and black, each group having a distinct social status. In the United States, on the other hand, there are but two groups, white and colored, or as the latter is now more frequently designated, Negro, the term thus losing its original meaning, and becoming a designation for a race. But while the white race usually makes no social distinction between the light and the dark Negro, classing all alike, social lines are drawn within the color line. Years ago these were more common than they are now. Charles W. Chesnutt, the novelist, tells some amusing and pathetic stories of distinctions between colored and black. One of his mulatto heroes, upon finding, as he thinks, that the congressman who is to call upon his daughter is a jet-black Negro instead of the mulatto he was supposed to be, to prevent a breach of hospitality, invents a case of diphtheria in the family and quarantines the house, only to learn later, to his intense mortification, that he has committed a mistake of identification, and that the congressman is light after all. But this story belongs with the last generation. Black men, if they are distinguished citizens, can enter any colored society, and they not infrequently marry light wives. Success, a position of probity and importance, these are attributes that count favorably for the suitor, and as they are quite as often in the man of strong African lineage as in the mulatto, they gain the desired end.

Within this little colored world of a few thousand souls, a drop in the city's human sea, there is great upheaval and turmoil. The North is the Negro's center for controversy regarding his rightful position in the commonwealth; and in the large cities, in Boston and Chicago, Philadelphia and New York, the battle rages. The little society is often divided into hostile camps regarding party politics or the acceptance of a government position that brings the suspicion of a bribe. Political, economic, educational matters as they affect the black race, these are the subjects that fill the mind of the thoughtful colored man and woman.

In his *Souls of Black Folk,* Dr. Du Bois describes the white man's tactlessness when, as always, he approaches the Negro with a question regarding his race. But the Negro, apart from his personal home affairs, impresses the outsider as having little else as subject for conversation. World politics, these concern him only as they affect the race question. Australia is a country where the government excludes Africans. England rules in South Africa and has lately recognized the right of African disfranchisement. Germany in Africa is cruel to black men. The Latin people know no color line. At home, the conflict of capital and labor is important as the Negro wins or loses in the economic struggle; the enfranchisement of woman is wise or unwise as it would affect Negro enfranchisement, one colored thinker arguing against it since it would double the white vote in the South where the Negro has no political rights; literature is the poetry of Dunbar, the writing of Washington and Du Bois, the literature of the Negro question, and art is largely comprised in Tanner's paintings.

This picture should not imply that the colored people of means are without the possibility of wide culture and sympathy. They are perhaps more sympathetic by nature than the white people about them. But each year, as the white American grows increasingly conscious of race, as he argues on racial differences, the Negro feels his dark face, is sensitive to every disdainful look, and separates himself from the people about him and their problems.

There is a struggle against this. The majority of white people have heard, in a vague way, that there is a difference of opinion in the Negro world; and again, vaguely, that it takes the form of opposition to Dr. Booker T. Washington and industrial training. But the difference of opinion among the Negroes is a difference of ideals, and reaches far beyond the controversy of industrial or cultural training, or the question of individual leadership. It is difficult to formulate, inasmuch as few, if any, Negroes hold logically to one ideal wholly to the exclusion of the other. They cannot be logical and live. But their division into radical and conservative is too important to omit; especially since, as we have seen, there is nothing in their social life to distinguish them from their neighbors; only in their thoughts are they aloof from us—aliens upon whose shoulders is the problem of a race.

How can one explain these two ideals? Roughly, they accept or reject segregation. The first looks upon the black man in America, for many generations at least, as a race apart. Recognizing this, the race must increasingly grow in self-efficiency. It must run its own businesses, own its banks, its groceries, its restaurants, have its dressmakers, milliners, tailors; it must establish factories where it shall employ only colored men and women; its children shall be brought into the world by colored doctors, taught by colored teachers, buried by colored undertakers. Education, along industrial lines, shall help train the worker to this efficiency, and a proper race pride shall give him the patronage of the Negroes about him. When, as will of course happen in the majority of cases, the Negro works for the white man, he must consider himself and his race. He must not go out on strike when the white man strives for higher wages; he is justified, if he is willing to risk a broken head, in filling the place of the striking workman, for he has to look after his own concerns.

The second point of view resists segregation. It believes that the Negro should never cease to struggle against being treated as a race apart, that he should demand the privileges of a citizen, free access to all public institutions, full civil and political rights. As a workman, he should have the opportunity of other workmen, his training should be the training of his white neighbor, and in business and the professions he should strive to serve white as well as black. And just as in the battlefield he fights in a common cause with his white comrade, so in the struggle for better working class conditions he should stand by the side of the laborer, regardless of race. Believing these things and finding that America fails to meet his demands, he thinks it should be his part to struggle for his ideal, vigorously to protest against discrimination, and never, complacent, to submit to the position of inferiority.

As I have said, few men hold logically to either of these ideals, and as that of acquiescence to present conditions is naturally popular with the whites, who are themselves responsible for discrimination, material success sometimes means a departure from the aggressive to the submissive attitude. However, the whole question of the Negro as a wage earner is yet scarcely understood by this small professional and business class. They are in turmoil, in a virile struggle, harsh, bewildering, baffling.

"I cannot conceive what it would mean not to be a Negro," a prominent New York colored man once said to me. "The white people think and feel so little; their life lacks an absorbing interest."

This is the characteristic fact of the life of the well-to-do Negro in New York. He is not permitted to go through the city streets in easy comfort of body or mind. Some personal rebuff, some harsh word in newspaper or magazine, quickens his pulse and rouses him from the lethargy that often overtakes his comfortable white neighbor. Looking into the past of slavery, watching the coming generation, the most careless of heart is forced into serious questioning. A comfortable income and the intelligence to enjoy the culture of a great city do not bring to the Negro any smug self-satisfaction; only a greater responsibility toward the problem that moves through the world with his dark face.

Before turning to our last topic, the Negro and the Municipality, we ought to note two further characteristics of the Negro in New York.

There are certan statistics quoted by every writer upon the Negro, statistics of mortality and crime. We have noted these for the child, but not as yet for the Negroes as a whole. They have been left until this point in our study that we may view them in relation to what we have learned of the Negro's economic condition and his environment.

Looking for criminal statistics first, we find them difficult to obtain in New York. The courts' reports do not classify by color, but we can learn something from the census enumeration of 1904 of the prisoners in the New York County Penitentiary and the New York County Workhouse. These are short-term offenders sent up from the city of New York. The enumeration is as follows:

NEW YORK COUNTY PENITENTIARY (BLACKWELL'S ISLAND)				
	Total	Males	Females	Per cent Total	Per cent Females
White	582	533	49	91.8	8.4
Colored	52	33	19	8.2	36.5

NEW YORK COUNTY WORKHOUSE				
White	1126	870	256	96.5	22.7
Colored	41	12	29	3.5	70.7

In view of the proportion of Negroes to whites in Manhattan, 2 per cent, we find the percentage of colored prisoners high, but no higher than we expect when we remember that the Negro occupies the lowest plane in the industrial community, "the plane which everywhere supplies the jail, the penitentiary, the gallows." [1] But the very large percentage of crime among colored women calls for grave consideration. In the workhouse, imprisoned for fighting, for drunkenness, for prostitution, the colored women more than double in number the colored men. Here is a condition that we noted in the Children's Court records: an unduly large percentage of disorderly and depraved colored female offenders.

We have already touched upon the subject of morality among colored women. Various causes, some of which we have noted, go to the making up of this high percentage of crime. The Negroes themselves believe the basic cause to be their recent enslavement with its attendant unstable marriage and parental status. They point to the centuries of healthful home relationships among Americans and Europeans, and contrast them with the thousands upon thousands of yearly sales of slaves that but

1. Quincy Ewing, "The Heart of the Race Problem," *Atlantic Monthly*, March, 1909.

two generations ago disrupted the Negro's attempts at family life. With this heritage they believe that it is inevitable that numbers of their women should be slow to recognize the sanctity of home and the importance of feminine virtue.

The mortality figures for the New York Negro are more striking than the figures for crime. In 1908 the death rate for whites in the city was 16.6 in every thousand; for colored (including Chinese), 28.9, almost double the white rate. The Negroes' greatest excess over the white was in tuberculosis, congenital debility, and venereal diseases as the following table shows.

New York, 1908	White	Colored
Number of deaths from all causes per 1000 population	16.6	28.9
Number of deaths per 1000 deaths:		
Tuberculosis	136	232.8
Pneumonia	126	136.3
Diarrhea and enteritis	91.8	79
Bright's disease	78.3	56.5
Heart disease	76.7	83.4
Cancer	45.5	24.8
Congenital debility	24.5	34.1
Diphtheria and croup	23.7	15
Scarlet fever	19	3.2
Typhoid	7.3	6.9
Venereal diseases	4	13.4
All others	367.2	314.6
	1000.0	1000.0

The Negro's inherent weakness, his inability to resist disease, is a favorite topic today with writers on the color question. A high mortality is indeed a matter for grave concern, but we may question whether these figures show inherent weakness. If a new disease attacks any group of people, it causes terrible decimation, and tuberculosis and venereal diseases, the white man's plagues, have proved terribly destructive to the black man. But recalling the conditions under which the great majority of the colored race lives in New York, the long hours of labor, the crowded rooms, the insufficient food, we find abundant cause for a high death rate. For poverty and death go hand in hand, and the proportion of Negroes in New York who live in great poverty far exceeds the proportion of whites.[2]

The students at Hampton Institute sing an old plantation song that runs like this:

> If religion was a thing that money could buy,
> The rich would live and the poor would die.
> But my good Lord has fixed it so
> The rich and the poor together must go.

Some of our rich men seem to have fixed it with religion to escape from the condition the poem describes, but it depicts a reality in the Negro's life. Rich and poor, as we saw when we left our old New Yorkers, competent and inefficient, pure and diseased, good and bad, all go together. Much of the recent literature written by Negroes, and especially that by Dr. Booker T. Washington, attempts to separate in the minds of the community the thrifty and prosperous colored men from the helpless and degraded; but the effort meets with a limited success. When we can

2. The statistician, Mr. I. B. Rubinow, in a discussion of high death rates (American Statistical Association, December, 1905) quotes the rate in five agricultural districts in a province of Russia, districts inhabited by peasantry of a common stock. With almost mathematical certainty, prosperity brings longer life. He divides his peasants into six groups showing their death rate as follows:

	Death Rate
Having no land	34.7
Less than 13.5 acres	32.7
13.5 to 40.5 acres	30.1
40.5 to 67.5 acres	25.4
67.5 acres to 135 acres	23.1
More than 135 acres	19.2

Mr. Rubinow suggests that the high Negro death rate may be explained by noting the poorly paid occupations in which the Negro engages.

have a statistical study of some thousands of the well-to-do Negroes compared with an equal number of well-to-do whites, we may find striking similarity. From my own observations I find that the well-to-do Negroes bear and rear children, refrain from committing crimes that put them into jail, and live to an old age with the same success as their white neighbors. But they get little credit for it. Willy-nilly, the strong, intellectual Negro is linked to his unfortunate fellow. Whether an increase in material prosperity will break this bond, or whether it will continue until it ceases to be a bond as humanity comes into its own, is a secret of the future. For today the song rings true, and the rich and the poor go together.

CHAPTER EIGHT

The Negro and
the Municipality

A CAPRICIOUS MOOD, varying with the individual, considerate today and offensive tomorrow, this, as far as our observations have led us, has been New York's attitude toward the Negro. Is it possible to find any principle underlying this shifting position? The city expresses itself through the individual actions of its changing four millions of people, but also through its government, its courts of justice, its manifold public activities. Out of these various manifestations of the community's spirit can we find a Negro policy? Has New York any principle of conduct toward these her colored citizens? This question should be worth our consideration, for New York's attitude means its environmental influence, and helps determine for the newly arrived immigrant and the growing generation whether justice or intolerance shall mark their dealings with the black race.

The first matter of civic importance to the Negro, as to every other New York resident, is his position in the commonwealth; is he a participant in the government under which he lives, or a subject without political rights? The law since 1873 has been explicit on this matter, wiping out former property qualifications, and giving full manhood suffrage. Probably, even with a much larger influx of colored people, the city will never agitate this question again. Since the death of the Know-nothing party, New York has ceased any organized attempt to lessen the power of the foreigner, and the growing cosmopolitan character of the population strengthens the Negro in his rights. Only in those states where the white population is homogeneous can Negro disfranchisement successfully take place.

With the vote the Negro has entered into politics and has maintained successful political organizations. The necessity of paying for rent and food out of eight or ten dollars a week is the Negro's immediate issue in New York, and he tries to meet it by securing a congenial and more lucrative job. The city in 1910 showed some consideration for him in this matter. An Assistant District Attorney and an Assistant Corporation Counsel were colored, and scattered throughout the city departments were nine clerks making from $1200 to $1800 apiece, and a dozen more acting as messengers, inspectors, drivers, attendants, receiving salaries averaging $1275. Three doctors served the Board of Health, and there were six men on the police force (none given patrol duty), and one first-grade fireman, while the departments of docks, parks, street cleaning, and water supply employed 470 colored laborers. Altogether 511 colored men figure among the city's employees.[1]

In her communal gifts the city acts toward the Negro with a fair degree of impartiality. At the public schools and libraries, the parks and playgrounds, the baths, hospitals, and, last, the almshouse, the blacks have equal rights with the whites. Occasionally individual public servants show color prejudice, but again, occasionally, especial kindness attends the black child. The rude treatment awaiting them, however, from other visitors keeps many Negro children, and men and women, from enjoying the city's benefactions. Particularly is this true with the public baths and with some of the playgrounds. The employment by the city of

1. The total number of municipal employees is 55,006—Negro employees, 511—Percentage of Negro to whole, 0.9.

at least one colored official in every neighborhood where the Negroes are in great numbers would do much to remedy this condition.

One department of the city might be cited as having been an exception to the rule of reasonably fair treatment to the colored man. Harshness, for no cause but his black face, has been too frequently bestowed upon the Negro by the police. This has been especially noticeable in conflicts between white and colored, when the white officer, instead of dealing impartially with offenders, protected his own race.

There have been two conflicts between the whites and Negroes in New York in recent years, the first in 1900, on the West Side, in the Forties, the second in 1905, on San Juan Hill. Each riot was local, representing no widespread excitement comparable to the draft riots of 1863, and in each case the police might easily in the beginning have stopped all fighting. Instead, they showed themselves ready to aid, even to instigate the conflict.

The riot of 1900 was caused by the death of a policeman at the hands of a Negro. The black man declared that he was defending his life, but the officer was popular, and after his funeral riots began. Black men ran to the police for protection, and were thrown back by them into the hands of the mob.[2]

The riot of 1905 commenced on San Juan Hill one Friday evening in July with a fracas between a colored boy and a white peddler; both races took a hand in the matter until the side streets showed a rough scrambling fight. Saturday and Sunday were comparatively quiet; men, black and white, stood on street corners and scowled at one another, but nothing further need have occurred, had each race been treated with justice. The police, however, instead of keeping the peace, angered the Negroes, urged on their enemies, and by Monday night found that they had helped create a riot, this time bitter and dangerous. Overzealous to proceed against the "niggers," officers rushed into places frequented by peaceable colored men, whom they placed under arrest. Drag-

2. *Story of the Riot,* published by Citizens Protective League.

ging their victims to the station house they beat them so unmercifully that before long many needed to be handed over to another city department—the hospital. Little question was made as to guilt or innocence, and some of the worst offenders, colored as well as white, were never brought to justice.[3] "If," as a colored preacher whose church was the center of the storm district pointed out, "the police would only differentiate between the good and the bad Negroes, and not knock on the head every colored man they saw in a riot, we should be quite satisfied. As it is, there is no safety for any Negro in this part of the city at any time." [4]

The result of these two riots was the bringing to justice of one policeman and the placing of a humane and tactful captain on San Juan Hill. But for some time the colored man felt little protection in the Department of Police, finding that he was liable to arrest and clubbing for a trivial offense. Often the officer's club fell with cruel force. This, however, was before the administration of Mayor Gaynor, who has commanded humane treatment, and the brutal clubbing of the New York Negro has now ceased.

From the police one turns naturally to the courts. What is their attitude toward the Negro offender? Is there any race prejudice, or do black and white enjoy an impartial and judicial hearing?

As the Negro comes before the magistrates of the city courts, he learns to know that judges differ greatly in their conceptions of justice. To the Southerner, let us say from Richmond, where the black man is arrested for small offenses and treated with considerable roughness and harshness, New York courts seem lenient.[5] To the West Indian, accustomed to British rule, justice

3. New York *Age,* July 27, 1905.

4. *New York Tribune,* July 24, 1905.

5. A Southern student says, "The Negro in Richmond is arrested for small offenses and fined in the city courts. He is treated with considerable roughness and harshness in his punishment for these offenses. It looks as though he were being imposed upon as an individual of the lower strata of society. But the Negro responds so impulsively to what appeals, that constant fear, dread, and impressiveness of the police act well as resistants to temptations."

in New York is noticeable for its variability, the likelihood that if it is severe tonight, it will be generous tomorrow.

"Three months," the listener at court hears given as sentence to a respectable-looking colored servant girl who has begged to be allowed to return to her place which she has held for five years. "I never was up for drinking before," she pleads; "I have learnt my lesson; please give me a chance; I will not do this again."

"What should you two be fighting for?" another judge, another morning, says to two very battered women, one white and one colored, who come before him in court. And talking kindly to both, but with greater seriousness to the Irish offender, his own countrywoman, he sends them away with a reprimand.

How much of this unequal treatment comes from color prejudice or caprice or temperament, the Negro is unable to decide, but he soon learns one curious fact: while his black skin marks him as inheriting Republican politics, it is the Democratic magistrate, the Tammany henchman whose name is a byword to the righteous, who is the more lenient when he has committed a trifling offense.

"Didn't I play craps with the nigger boys when I was a kid?" one of these well-known politicians says, "and am I going back on the poor fellows now?" Of course, the Negro is assured such men only want his vote, but he believes real sympathy actuates the Tammany leader, who is too busy to bother whether the man before him is black or white. The reformer, on the other hand, big with dignity, at times makes him vastly uncomfortable as he lectures upon the Negro problem from the eminence of the superior race.

But whether Republican or Democrat, the Negro learns that it is well to have a friend at court; that helplessness is the worst of all disabilities, worse than darkness of skin or poverty. So he soon becomes acquainted with his local politician, and if his friend is in trouble, or his wife or son is locked up, pounds vigorously at the politician's door. It may be midnight, but the man of power will dress, and together they will turn from the dark tenement hall into the lighted street and on to the police station or magistrate's court to seek release for the offender. That too often the gravity of the offense weighs little in the securing of lenient treatment is part of the muddle of New York justice. The Negro finds that he has taken the most direct way to secure relief.

As far as we have followed, we have found the municipality of New York generally ready to treat her black citizens with the same justice or injustice with which she treats her whites. Exceptions occur, but she does not often draw the color line. Perhaps, in this connection, it might be well to stop a moment and see what return the black man makes, whether by his vote he helps secure to the city honest and efficient government.

Walking through a Negro quarter on election day, the most careful search fails to reveal any such farsighted altruism. With a great majority of colored voters the choice of a municipal candidate is based on the argument of a two-dollar bill or the promise of a job, combined with the sentiment, decreasing every year, for the Republican party—the party that once helped the colored man and, he hopes, may help him again. The public standing of the mayoralty candidate, his ability to choose wise heads of departments, the building of new subways, the ownership of public utilities, these are unimportant issues. The matter of immediate moment is what this vote is going to mean to the black voter himself.

Such a selfish and unpatriotic attitude, not unknown perhaps to white voters, leads some of our writers and reformers to doubt the value of universal manhood suffrage. Mr. Ray Stannard Baker tells us that the Negro and the poor white in New York, through their venality, are practically without a vote. "While the South is disfranchising by legislation," he says, "the North is doing it by cash. What else is the meaning of Tammany Hall and the boss and machine system in other cities?" [6] New York's noted ethical culture teacher argues against agitation for women's suffrage on the ground that so many of those who now have the vote do not know

6. Ray Stannard Baker, *Following the Color Line*, p. 269.

how to use it. But looking closely at these unaltruistic citizens, we see that after all they are putting the ballot to its primary use, the protection of their own interests. The Negro in New York has one vital need, steady, decent work. He dickers and plays with politics to get as much of this as he can. It is very insufficient relief for an intolerable situation, but it is partial relief. In another city, Atlanta for instance, he might find education the most important civic gift for which to strive. Atlanta is a fortunate city to choose for an example of the power of the suffrage, for since the Negro's loss of the vote in Georgia, educational funds have been turned chiefly to white schools, and 5,000 colored children are without opportunities for public education. 1885 saw the last school building erected for Negroes, the result of a bargain between the colored voters and the prohibitionists.[7] Should a colored teacher in New York be refused her certificate, a colored consumptive be denied a place in the city's hospital, a colored

7. The following story of Athens, Georgia, told by a Northerner teaching in the South, illustrates this point. "The city of Athens was planning to inaugurate a public school system, and also wished to 'go dry.' It made a proposal to the colored voters promising that if their combined vote would carry the city, two schools should be built, of equal size and similar structure for each race. I visited Athens shortly after the two buildings were built, and I found two beautiful brick buildings very similar in all their appointments. At an interval of several years I again visited the little city and again spent an hour in the same brick schoolhouse of the colored folk.

"At my third visit, I found my colored friends occupying a wooden structure on the edge of the city, and not only inconveniently located, but much less of a building than the one hitherto occupied. Upon inquiry I found that in the growth of the school population of the whites, it was cheaper to seize the building formerly occupied by the colored children, and to build for them a cheap wooden structure on the outskirts of the town.

"The colored school was still occupying this inadequate building at my visit this last September, 1909. A second wooden structure has been added to the colored equipment on the east side of the town."

This story of the Athenians well illustrates what will be done when the Negro counts for something politically, and also what may be undone if his value as a political asset is reduced.

child meet with a rebuff in the city park, the colored citizen would find his vote an important means of redress. Then, too, while there are so many men to buy, it is important to have a vote to sell, lest the other citizens secure the morning's bargains. Venality in high and low places will not disappear until we are dominated by the ideal of social, not individual advancement. Before that time, it is well for the weak that they are able, at least in the political field, to bargain with the strong.

The importance to the Negro of the vote is quickly appreciated when we consider New York's attitude unofficially expressed. With the franchise behind him the colored man can secure for himself and his children the municipality's advantages of education, health, amusement, philanthropy. He is here a citizen, a contributor to the city treasury, if not directly as a taxpayer, as a worker and renter. But as a private individual, seeking to use the utilities managed by other private individuals, he continually encounters race discrimination. Private doors are closed, and were the state not so wealthy and generous, disabilities still graver than at present would follow.

A few examples will show the condition. A Negro applies by letter for admission to an automobile school, and is accepted; but on appearing with his fee his color debars his entrance. Carrying the case to court, the complaint is dismissed on the ground that the law which forbade exclusion from places of education on account of race and color is applicable only to public schools. Private institutions may do as they desire.

Again, a colored man tries to get a meal. At the first restaurant he is told that all the tables are engaged; at the next no one will serve him. Fearful of further rebuffs, he has to turn to the counter of a railway station. He wants to go to the theater. Like Tommy Atkins, he is sent to the gallery or round the music halls. The white barber whose shop he enters will not shave him; and when night comes, he searches a long time before the hotel appears that will give him a bed. The sensitive man, still more the sensitive woman, often finds the city's attitude difficult to endure.

American Negroes have become familiar with racial lines, but the foreigner of African descent, a visitor to the city, meets with rebuffs that fill him with surprise as well as rage. Haitians and South Americans, men of continental education and wide culture, have been ordered away as "niggers" from restaurant doors, and at the box office of the theater refused an orchestra seat. English Negroes from the West Indies, men and women of character and means, learn that New York is a spot to be avoided, and cross the ocean when they wish to taste of city life. In short, the stranger of Negro descent, if he be rash of temper, hurls anathemas at the villainously mannered Americans; or, if he be good-natured, shrugs his shoulders and counts New York a provincial settlement of four million people.

Northern Negroes believe this discrimination in public places against the black man to be increasing in New York. One, who came here fifteen years ago, tells of the simple and adequate test by which he learned that he had reached the Northern city. Born in South Carolina, as he attained manhood he desired larger self-expression, broader human relations—he wanted "to be free," as he again and again expressed it. So leaving the cotton fields he started one morning to walk to New York. After a number of days he entered a large city and, uncertain in his geography, decided that this was his journey's end. "I'll be free here," he thought, and opening the door of a brightly lighted restaurant started to walk in. The white men at the tables looked up in astonishment, and the proprietor, laying his hand on the youth's shoulder, invited him, in strong Southern accent, to go into the kitchen. "I reckon I'm not North yet," the Negro said, smiling a bright, boyish smile. Interested in his visitor's appearance, the proprietor took him into another room, gave him a good supper, and talked with him far into the night, urging the advantages of his staying in the South. But the youth shook his head, and the next morning trudged on. At length he reached a rushing city, tumultuous with humanity, and entering an eating house was served a meal. To him it was almost a sacrament. He belonged not to a race but to humanity. He tasted the freedom of passing unnoticed. But it is doubtful if the same restaurant would serve him today.

Color lines, on these matters of entertainment as on others, are not hard and fast. A few hotels, chiefly those frequented by Latin peoples, receive colored guests; and while the foreign Negro meets with rudeness, he is rebuffed less than the native. "I can't get into that place as a Southern darky," a black man laughingly says, pointing to a fashionable restaurant, "I'll be the Prince of Abyssinia." But as Prince or American his status is shifting and uncertain; here, pre-eminently, he is half a man.

Discrimination against any man because of his color is contrary to the law of the state. After the fifteenth amendment became a law, New York passed a civil rights bill, which as it stands, re-enacted in 1909, is very explicit. All persons within the jurisdiction of the state are entitled to the accommodation of hotels, restaurants, theaters, music halls, barbers' shops, and any person refusing such accommodation is subject to civil and penal action. The offense may be punished by fine or imprisonment or both.[8]

8. Civil Rights Law, State of New York. Chapter 14 of the Laws of 1909, being Chapter 6 of the Consolidated Laws.

"Article 4.—Equal rights in places of public amusement.

"Section 40.—All persons within the jurisdiction of this state shall be entitled to the full and equal accommodations, advantages, facilities, and privileges of inns, restaurants, hotels, eating houses, bath houses, barber shops, theatres, music halls, public conveyances on land and water, and all other places of public accommodation or amusement, subject only to the conditions and limitations, established by the law and applicable alike to all citizens.

"Section 41.—Penalty for violation. Any person who shall violate any of the provisions of the foregoing section by denying to any citizen, except for reasons applicable alike to all citizens of every race, creed and color, and regardless of race, creed and color, the full enjoyment of any of the accommodations, advantages, facilities or privileges in said section enumerated, or by aiding or inciting such denial, shall, for every such offense, forfeit and pay a sum not less than one hundred dollars nor more than five hundred dollars to the person aggrieved thereby, to be recovered

In 1888, the attempt to exclude three colored men from a skating rink at Binghamton, N. Y., led to a suit against the owner of the rink, and his conviction. The case[9] reached the Court of Appeals, where the constitutionality of the civil rights bill was upheld. "It is evident," said Justice Andrews in his decision, "that to exclude colored people from places of public resort on account of their race is to fix upon them a brand of inferiority, and tends to fix their position as a servile and dependent people."

But despite the law and precedent, the civil rights bill is violated in New York. Occasionally colored men bring suit, but the magistrate dismisses the complaint. Usually the evidence is declared insufficient. A case of a colored man refused orchestra seats at a theater is dismissed on the ground that not the proprietor but his employees turned the man away. A keeper of an ice-cream parlor, wishing to prevent the colored man from patronizing him, charges a Negro a dollar for a ten-cent plate. The customer pays the dollar, keeps the check, and brings the case to court. Ice-cream parlors are then declared not to come under the list of places of public entertainment and amusement. A bootblack refuses to polish the shoes of a Negro, and the court decides that a bootblack stand is not a place of public accommodation, and refusal to shine the shoes of a colored man does not subject its proprietor to the penalties imposed by the law.[10] This last case was carried to the Court of Appeals, and the adverse judgment has led many of the thoughtful colored men of the city to doubt the value of attempting to push a civil rights suit. Litigation is expensive, and money spent in any personal rights case that attacks private

in a court of competent jurisdiction in the County where said offense was committed, and shall also, for every such offense, be deemed guilty of a misdemeanor, and upon conviction thereof shall be fined not less than one hundred dollars nor more than five hundred dollars, or shall be imprisoned not less than thirty days nor more than ninety days, or both such fine and imprisonment."

9. People *v*. King, 110 N. Y., 418, 1888.

10. Burke *v*. Bosso, 180 N. Y., 341, 1905.

business, whether the plaintiff be white or colored, is usually wasted. The civil rights law is on the books, and the psychological moment may arrive to insist successfully on its enforcement.

If there is an increase in discrimination against the Negro in New York solely because of his color, it is a serious matter to the city as well as to the race. Every community has its social conscience built up of slowly accumulated experiences, and it cannot without disaster lose its ideal of justice or generosity. New York has never been tender to its people, but it has a rough hospitality, what Stevenson describes as "uncivil kindness," and welcomes newcomers with a friendly shove, bidding them become good Americans. After the war, the Negro entered more than formerly into this general welcome. He was unnoticed, allowed to go his way without questioning word or stare, the position which every right-minded man and woman desires. But today New York has become conscious that he is dark-skinned, and her attitude affects her growing children. "I never noticed colored people," an old abolitionist said to me. "I never realized there were white and black until, when a boy of twelve, I entered a church and found Negroes occupying seats alone in the gallery." As New York returns to the gallery seats, her boys and girls return to consciousness of color and, from fisticuffs at school, move on to the race riots upon the streets with bullets among the stones.

The municipality, as we have seen, treats the Negro on the whole with justice; its standard is higher than the standard of the average citizen. It cherishes the ideal of democracy, and strives for impartiality toward its many nationalities and races. And the New York Negro in his turn does not allow his liberties to be tampered with without protest. But the New York citizen can hardly be described as friendly to the Negro. What catholicity he has is negative. He fails to give the black man a hearty welcome. "Do you know where I stayed the four weeks of my first trip abroad?" a colored clergyman once asked me. I refused to make a guess. "Well," he said a little shamefacedly, "it was in Paris. Paris may be a wicked city—any city has wickedness if you want to look for it—but I found it a place of kindliness and good will. Everyone seemed glad to be courteous, to assist me in my stumbling French, to show me the way on omnibus or boat, or through the difficult streets. It was so different from America; I was never wanted in the Southern city of my youth. In Paris I was welcome."

"How is it in New York?" I asked.

"In New York?" He stopped to consider. "In New York I am tolerated."

CHAPTER NINE

Conclusion

A NEW LITTLE BOY came two years ago into our storybook world. When Miss North, taking Ezekiel by the hand, led him into her schoolroom,[1] we met a child full of what we call temperament; dreaming quaint stories, innocently friendly, anxious to please for affection's sake, in his queer, unconscious way something of a genius. We saw his big musing eyes looking out upon a world in which his teacher stood serene and reasoning, but a little cold like her name; his friend, Miss Jane, kind and very practical; his employer, Mr. Rankin, amused and contemptuous; all watching him with the impersonal interest with which one might view a new species in the animal world. For Ezekiel, unlike our other storybook boys, had a double being, he was first Ezekiel Jordan, a little black boy, and second, a representative of the Negro race.

Ezekiel was too young to understand his position, but the white world about him never forgot it. When he arrived late to school, he was a dilatory representative; when, obliging little soul, he promised three people to weed their gardens all the same after-

1. Lucy Pratt, *Ezekiel* (Boston and New York: Houghton Mifflin Company, 1914).

120

noon, he was a prevaricating representative. He never happened to steal ice cream from the hoke-poke man or to play hookey, but if he had, he would have been a thieving and lazy representative. Always he was something remote and overwhelming, not a natural growing boy.

Ezekiel's position is that of each Negro child and man and woman in the United States today. I think we have seen this as we have reviewed the position of the race in New York; indeed, the very fact of our attempting such a review is patent that we see and feel it. We white Americans do not generalize concerning ourselves, we individualize, leaving generalizations to the chance visitor, but we generalize continually concerning colored Americans; we classify and measure and pass judgment, a little more with each succeeding year.

Now if we are going to do this, let us be fair; let us try as much as possible to dismiss prejudice, and to look at the Ezekiels entering our school of life, with the same impartiality and the same understanding sympathy with which we look upon our own race. And if we are to place them side by side with the whites, let us be impartial, not cheating them out of their hard-earned credits, or condemning them with undue severity. Let us try, if we can, to be just.

When we begin to make this effort to judge fairly our colored world, we need to remember especially two things: First, that we cannot yet measure with any accuracy the capability of the colored man in the United States, because he has not yet been given the opportunity to show his capability. If we deny full expression to a race, if we restrict its education, stifle its intellectual and aesthetic impulses, we make it impossible fairly to gauge its ability. Under these circumstances to measure its achievements with the more favored white race is unreasonable and unjust, as unreasonable as to measure against a man's a disfranchised woman's capabilities in directing the affairs of a state.[2]

2. "The world of modern intellectual life is in reality a white man's world. Few women and perhaps no blacks have entered this world in the

The second thing is difficult for us to remember, difficult for us at first to believe; that we, dominant, ruling Americans, may not be the persons best fitted to judge the Negro. We feel confident that we are, since we have known him so long and are so familiar with his peculiarities; but in moments of earnest reflection may it not occur to us that we have not the desire or the imagination to enter into the life emotions of others? "We are the intellect and virtue of the airth, the cream of human natur', and the flower of moral force," Hannibal Chollup still says, and glowers at the stranger who dares to suggest a different standard from his own. Hannibal Chollup and his ilk are ill fitted to measure the refinements of feeling, the differences in ideals among people.

This question of our fitness to sit in the judgment seat must come with grave insistence when we read carefully the literature published in this city of New York within the past two years. Our writers have assumed such pomposity, have so reveled in what Mr. Chesterton calls "the magnificent buttering of one's self all over with the same stale butter; the big defiance of small enemies," as to make their conclusions ridiculous. Ezekiel entering their school is at once pushed to the bottom of the class, while the white boy at the head, Hannibal Chollup's descendant, sings a jubilate of his own and butters himself so copiously as to be as shiny as his English cousin, Wackford Squeers. Then the writer, the judge, begins. Ezekiel is shown as the incorrigible boy of the school. He is a lazy, good-for-nothing vagabond. Favored with the chance to exercise his muscles twelve hours a day for a disinterested employer, he fails to appreciate his

---

fullest sense. To enter it in the fullest sense would be to be in it at every moment from the time of birth to the time of death, and to absorb it unconsciously and consciously, as the child absorbs language. When something like this happens we shall be in a position to judge of the mental efficiency of women and the lower races. At present we seem justified in inferring that the differences in mental expression between the higher and lower races and between men and women are no greater than they should be in view of the existing differences in opportunity." W. I. Thomas, *Sex and Society*, p. 312.

opportunity. He is diseased, degenerate. His sisters are without chastity, every one, polluting the good, pure white men about them. He is a rapist, and it is his criminal tendencies that are degrading America. The pale-faced ones of his family steal into white society, marry, and insinuate grasping, avaricious tendencies into the noble, generous men of white blood, causing them to cheat in business and to practice political corruption. In short there is nothing evil that Ezekiel is not at the bottom of. Sometimes, poor little chap, he tries to sniffle out a word, to say that his family is doing well, that he has an uncle who is buying a home, and a rich cousin in the undertaking business, but such extenuating circumstances receive scant attention, and we are not surprised to find, the class dismissed, that Ezekiel and the millions whom he represents, are swiftly shuffled off the earth, victims of "disease, vice, and profound discouragement."

Now this is not an exaggerated picture of much that has recently been printed in newspaper and magazine, and does it not make us feel the paradox that if we are to judge the Negro fairly, we must not judge him at all, so little are we temperamentally capable of meeting the first requirement?

"My brother Saxons," says Matthew Arnold, "have a terrible way with them of wanting to improve everything but themselves off the face of the earth." And he adds, "I have no such passion for finding nothing but myself everywhere." Among our American writers a few, like Arnold, do not care to find only themselves everywhere, and these have told us a different story of the American Negro. They are poets and writers of fiction, men and women who are happy in meeting and appreciating different types of human beings.[3] If these writers were to instruct us, they would say that we must individualize more when we think of the black people about us, must differentiate. That, too, we must remember that when we pass judgment, we need to know whether our own standard is the best, whether we may not have some-

3. Note especially the stories of Alice MacGowan and Grace Mac-Gowan Cooke, and the poems of Rosalie M. Jonas.

thing to learn from the standards of others. Supposing Ezekiel is deliberate and slow to make changes or to take risks; are we who are "acceleration mad," who acquire heart disease hustling to catch trains, who mortage our farms to buy automobiles, who seek continually new sensations, really better than he? Is it not a matter of difference, just as we may each place in different order our desires, the one choosing struggle for power and the accumulation of wealth, the other preferring serenity and pleasure in the immediate present? And lastly, after having praised our own virtues and our own ideals, must we not beware that we do not blame the Negro when he adopts them, that we do not turn upon him and fiercely demand only servile virtues, the virtues that make him useful not to himself but to us? [4]

No one can talk for long of the Negro in America without propounding the all-embracing question, What will become of him, what will be the outcome of all this racial controversy? It is a daring person who attempts to answer. We, who have studied the Negro in New York, may perhaps venture to predict a little regarding his future in this city, his possible status in the later years of the century; whether he will lose in opportunity and social position, or whether he will advance in his struggle to be a man.

Looking upon the great population of the city, its varied races and nationalities, I confess that his outlook to me begins to be bright. New York is still to a quite remarkable extent dominated socially by its old American stock, its Dutch and Anglo-Saxon

---

4. Careful readers of economic Negro studies by white writers will notice this tendency to look upon the Negro as belonging to a servile class. Emphasis is laid upon his responsibilities to the white man, not upon the white man's responsibilities to him. Anyone familiar with the sympathetic attitude toward the workers in such a study as the *Pittsburg Survey* will notice at once the difference in attitude in Negro surveys by whites, the slight emphasis laid upon the black laborers, long hours and poor pay, and the failure to emphasize the white man's responsibility. Negro laborers are still studied from the viewpoint of the capitalist. There is one notable exception to this, the study by the governor of Jamaica, Sir Sidney Olivier, on "White Capital and Coloured Labor."

element. Few things strike the foreign visitor so forcibly as that despite its enormous European population, American society is homogeneous. But this is not likely to continue for very long. When the present demand for exhausting self-supporting work becomes less insistent, we shall feel in a deeper, more vital way the influence of our vast foreign life. With a million Jews and nearly a million Latin peoples, we cannot for long be held in the provincialism of today. I suspect that to many Europeans New York seems still a great overgrown village in "a nation of villagers," pronouncing with narrow, dogmatic assurance upon the deep unsolved problems of life. But in the future it may take on a larger, more cosmopolitan spirit. Its Italians may bring a finer feeling for beauty and wholesome gaiety, its Jews may continue to add great intellectual achievements, and its people of African descent, perhaps always few in number, may show with happy spontaneity their best and highest gifts. If New York really becomes a cosmopolitan city, let us believe the Negro will bring to it his highest genius and will walk through it simply, quietly, unnoticed, a man among men.

Appendix

THE FEDERAL CENSUS in 1900 contained a volume on the Negro in the United States, a source of information quoted by nearly every writer on the American Negro. The tables in that volume, however, do not classify by cities, and any one desiring information regarding the Negro in some especial city must search through other volumes. As this is a lengthy task, I am affixing a list of the tables in the census of 1900, treating of the Negro in New York City, believing that it may also be a guide to students of the new census of 1910, who wish to find New York Negro statistics.

Population. Vol. I, Part I. Published 1901.

Page 868, Table 57. Aggregate, white, and colored population distributed according to native or foreign parentage, for cities having 25,000 inhabitants or more: 1900.

Page 934, Table 81. Total males twenty-one years of age and over, classified by general nativity, color, and literacy, for cities having 25,000 inhabitants or more: 1900.

Vol. II. Published 1902.

Page 163, Table 19. Persons of school age, five to twenty years, inclusive, by general nativity and color, for cities having 25,000 inhabitants or more: 1900. Also, pages 165 and 167, Tables 20 and 21.

Page 332, Table 32. Conjugal condition of the aggregate population, classified by sex, general nativity, color, and age periods, for cities having 100,000 inhabitants or more: 1900.

Page 397, Table 54. Negro persons attending school during the census year, classified by sex and age periods, for cities having 25,000 inhabitants or more: 1900.

Page 737, Table 111. Persons owning and hiring their homes, classified by color, for cities having 100,000 inhabitants or more: 1900.

Vital Statistics. Vol. III. Published 1902.

Page 458, Table 19. Population, births, deaths, and death rates at certain ages, and deaths from certain causes, by sex, color, general nativity, and parent nativity: census year 1900.

Occupations. Published 1904.

Pages 634 to 642, Table 43. Total males and females, ten years of age and over, engaged in selected groups of occupations, classified by general nativity, color, conjugal condition, months unemployed, age periods, and parentage, for cities having 50,000 inhabitants or more: 1900.

Supplementary Analysis. Published 1906.

Page 262, Table 87. Per cent Negro in total population, 1900, 1890, and 1889, per cent male and female in Negro population, per cent illiterate in Negro population at least ten years of age, and among Negro males of voting age, and per 10,000 distribution of Negro population by age periods.

Women at Work. Published 1907.

Page 146, Table 9. Number and percentage of breadwinners in female population, sixteen years of age and over, classified by race and nativity, for cities having at least 50,000 inhabitants: 1900.

Pages 147 to 151, Table 10. Number and percentage of breadwinners in the female population, sixteen years and over, classified by age, race, and nativity.

Pages 266 to 275, Table 28. Female breadwinners, sixteen years of age and over, classified by family relationship, and by race, nativity, marital condition, and occupation, for selected cities: 1900.

Pages 354 to 365, Table 29. Female breadwinners, sixteen years of

128   Appendix

age and over, living at home, classified by the number of other bread-winners in the family, and by race, nativity, marital condition, and occupation, for selected cities: 1900.

Mortality Statistics. Published 1908.

Page 28. Number of deaths from all causes per 1000 of population.

Page 376, Table 2. Deaths in each registration area, by age: 1908.

Pages 566 to 568, Table 8. Deaths in each city having 100,000 population or over in 1900, from certain causes and classes of causes, by age: 1908.

GLOBETROTTER™

Travel Guide

PERU

ROBIN GAULDIE

NEW
HOLLAND

NEW
HOLLAND

★★★ Highly recommended
★★ Recommended
★ See if you can

Second edition published in 2009
by New Holland Publishers (UK) Ltd
London • Cape Town • Sydney • Auckland
10 9 8 7 6 5 4 3 2 1

website: www.newhollandpublishers.com

Garfield House, 86 Edgware Road
London W2 2EA
United Kingdom

80 McKenzie Street
Cape Town 8001
South Africa

Unit 1, 66 Gibbes Street
Chatswood NSW 2067
Australia

218 Lake Road
Northcote, Auckland
New Zealand

Distributed in the USA by
The Globe Pequot Press, Connecticut

ISBN 978 1 84773 304 7

Keep us Current
Information in travel guides is apt to change, which is
why we regularly update our guides. We'd be grateful
to receive feedback if you've noted something we
should include in our updates. If you have new
information, please share it with us by writing to
the Publishing Manager, Globetrotter, at the office
nearest to you (addresses on this page). The most
significant contribution to each new edition will
receive a free copy of the updated guide.

Publishing Manager: Thea Grobbelaar
DTP Cartographic Manager: Geneé Hart
Editors: Carla Zietsman, Thea Grobbelaar
Design and DTP: Nicole Bannister
Cartographers: Carryck Wise, Tanja Spinola
Picture Researcher: Shavonne Govender

Reproduction by Unifoto, Cape Town and Resolution
(Cape Town)
Printed and bound by Times Offset (M) Sdn. Bhd.,
Malaysia

This guidebook has been written by independent
authors and updaters. The information therein represents their impartial opinion, and neither they nor the
publishers accept payment in return for including in
the book or writing more favourable reviews of any
of the establishments. Whilst every effort has been
made to ensure that this guidebook is as accurate
and up to date as possible, please be aware that the
facts quoted are subject to change, particularly the
price of food, transport and accommodation. The
Publisher accepts no responsibility or liability for any
loss, injury or inconvenience incurred by readers or
travellers using this guide.

Acknowledgements:
Robin Gauldie would like to thank American Airlines,
Guerba Expeditions, Latin America Travel, and
Promperu for their assistance in researching this guide.

Photographic Credits:
Tom Cockrem: pages 9, 26 (top), 30, 34, 35, 37, 39,
94, 98, 99, 101, 103, 112, 114; **Robin Gauldie:** pages
16, 19, 24, 26 (bottom), 42, 50, 52, 53, 64, 67, 68,
69, 70, 72, 74, 80, 81, 82, 83, 84, 85, 88, 89, 102;
Mike Langford: title page, pages 7, 10, 11, 12, 13, 14,
15, 28, 29, 32, 51, 55, 57, 58, 59, 60, 78, 91, 116,
117, 118, 119; **Larry Luxner:** pages 8, 17, 18, 21, 22,
23, 25, 27, 38, 41, 46, 76, 77; **Buddy Mays:** pages 4,
6, 61, 108; **Pictures Colour Library:** cover; **Richard
Sale:** pages 49, 54, 56; **South American Pictures/
Robert Francis:** pages 106, 107, 109; **South American
Pictures/Kathy Jarvis:** page 97; **South American
Pictures/Anna McVittie:** pages 43, 79, 104; **South
American Pictures/Kimball Morrison:** page 90; **South
American Pictures/Marion Morrison:** page 87; **South
American Pictures/Tony Morrison:** pages 36, 105.

Cover: *Machu Pichu, ancient Inca site.*
Title Page: *A Peruvian woman in traditional dress.*